FATHER FRANK PARRISH, S.J.

Sparks from His Heart

The Mystical
Humanity
of Christ
Publishing

San Mateo
2016
Second Edition

IMPRIMI POTEST
Paul F. Belcher, S.J.
Provincial of the California Province

NIHIL OBSTAT
Joseph Pollard, STD
Censor Deputatus

IMPRIMATUR
+ Roger Cardinal Mahony, D.D.
Archbishop of Los Angeles
Los Angeles, CA, February 7, 1991

Visit our Websites at CoraEvans.com and ParishRetreat.org

Cover design by Claudine Mansour Design, Mission Viejo, California
Interior design by Sherry Russell Design, Pasadena, California
Printed in the United States of America

Library of Congress Cataloging-in-Publication Data
Father Frank Parrish, S.J.
Sparks from His Heart

ISBN Paperback 978-0-9910506-5-9
ISBN eBook 978-0-9910506-6-6

FATHER FRANK'S STATEMENT OF APPRECIATION

For all those who have helped me by their inspiration and prayers through the years I am deeply grateful, particularly to Sal Maiorino.

RECOGNITION

The Mystical Humanity of Christ, Inc.
Gratefully acknowledges the Extraordinary Generosity
of the
Theresa and Edward O'Toole Foundation
Bert Degheri, Co-Trustee

APPRECIATION

The Society of Jesus and the Jesuits of the California Province
Fr. Michael Weiler, S.J., Provincial

PUBLISHER'S ACKNOWLEDGEMENTS

We express appreciation to June Haver MacMurray (deceased), and Fred and June MacMurray Foundation, Kate MacMurray, Al Marsella, Msgr. Padraic Loftus, Joe Berberich, Irene and Mark Montgomery, Don Ryan, Rob Smith, Peter Marlow Jr., Gabrielle Lien, and her late husband, Warren. Fr. Vito Perrone, COSJ, and Fr. Gary Thomas for their spiritual support and advice, Rob Bussell (deceased) for his inspiration and participation, Michael Huston, advisor, retreat leader and board member, and Pamela McDevitt, for her encouragement and guidance.

DEDICATION

The publisher recognizes the exemplary priesthood of Fr. Frank Parrish, S.J. who entrusted us with the writings of Cora Evans and the responsibility to promulgate the Mystical Humanity of Christ. It is an honor to publish his works.

PUBLISHER'S NOTE

The author, Father Frank Parrish, S.J., entered the Jesuits in 1929 and was ordained at Old Saint Mary's in San Francisco on June 13, 1942. Father Frank became the Los Angeles Archdiocesan Director of the Apostleship of Prayer and the League of the Sacred Heart, a responsibility that he held for 50 years. He was archdiocesan director for ministry to the deaf. He coached football, basketball, and swimming while teaching theology at Loyola High School. Later, he was dean of students at Loyola Marymount University.

He served as director of Manresa Retreat House 1965 to 1970 and became superior of the Colombiere House, a Jesuit residence in Los Angeles. His other ministries included:

Chaplin of Knights of Columbus, State of California
Chaplin of Catholic Daughters of the Americas
Chaplin of the Boy Scouts, honored as Distinguished Eagle Scout
Nationally syndicated Catholic television program, *Heart of the Nation*
Radio host for 50 years, "Catholic Quarter Hour"
Special recognition by The Mary and Joseph League
Author of *Sparks from His Heart*

Father Frank was spiritual director and confessor for the Catholic mystic Cora Evans from 1945 until her death in 1957. He founded the Mystical Humanity of Christ, Inc., an organization dedicated to continuing the mission entrusted to Cora Evans by our Lord: to promulgate the Mystical Humanity of Christ, the divine indwelling, as a way of prayer throughout the world. The cause for canonization of Servant of God Cora Evans is underway.

Among Catholics, Father Frank is perhaps best known for blessing terminally ill Father John A. Houle, S.J., with the relic of Blessed Claude La Colombière on February 23, 1990. This blessing led to a miraculous cure, a first-class miracle—the miracle needed for the final step in the sainthood process. Colombière was declared a saint and canonized by John Paul II on May 31, 1992. It is important to recognize both the extraordinary connection and obvious divine providence of this event in the life of Father Frank. Saint Claude La Colombière, also a Jesuit, was the spiritual director for Saint Margaret Mary Alacoque (1647–1690), the French nun who promoted the devotion to the Sacred Heart of Jesus and a mystic much like Cora Evans.

Father Frank passed away on December 29, 2003. We are pleased to publish this second edition of *Sparks from His Heart*, the first of a series of books featuring the writings of an exemplary priest for our time.

INTRODUCTION

Through the years of my priesthood, I have been engaged in giving many radio and television talks through "The Sacred Heart Program," "The Catholic Quarter Hour," and *Heart of the Nation*. The thought came to me of perpetuating these short sermonettes by putting them into book form. Perhaps those who read these "Sparks from His Heart" will feel the impact of our Divine Savior's love for them a little keener, and from them be shown how to return their love for Him.

The material has come from my personal meditations and experiences, readings of others, and the many retreats I have made and conducted through the years for men and women, married couples, and young people.

It is a great joy to me that during my jubilee of 50 years as a Jesuit priest, Saint Claude La Colombière was canonized by Pope John Paul II on May 31, 1992.

May our loving Savior, Jesus Christ, bless you as you read these words, and may He keep you forever in His Sacred Heart.

— Father Frank Parrish, S.J.

Contents

The Sacred Heart—
Burning Furnace of Love

NO TRUER WORDS were ever penned than those by the poet who wrote, "It's love that makes the world go 'round."

In the devotion to the Sacred Heart of Jesus, this driving power of love is lifted out of the quagmire of confusion and debasement—as it is harmfully and wrongly thought of by so many today—and placed on the lofty spiritual and supernatural heights of God Himself.

Devotion to the Sacred Heart is not something out on the periphery of Catholic life. It is not a "fringe" devotion in the Church—a sort of an unnecessary accident—but it is at the core of our Faith, by the very fact that it deals with the mystery of our divine Savior's love. As a matter of fact, this devotion is most characteristic of Christianity because it is devotion to Jesus Christ Himself represented by the most essential organ of His humanity, His Sacred Heart, which is the natural symbol of His love, both human and divine.

What is this love of which we speak? In answer I reply: it is the source of vital life to our Christian Faith. If the words of Saint John, "God is love"(Jn 4:16), were not true, then none of us would have come into existence, nor would there be an everlasting dwelling place for us with Him in Heaven.

So when we say that it is love which makes the world go 'round, we might add that without love none of us would have ever come into this world, been adopted as children of God, or be destined to enjoy eternal beatitude with Him. The love of our Savior, Jesus Christ, for each one of us, at Bethlehem, Nazareth, Jerusalem, and Calvary throughout His entire life, Passion, and death is beautifully and most naturally symbolized by His Sacred Heart. In it is contained everything, for it speaks not so much what Christ has done for us, but why he did it—and this why is summarized in one word, love. Everything from the first moment of His conception to His dying gasp on the cross was dominated by the one impelling motive of love.

Today, how can we return our love to Christ for all He has done for us? The Apostleship of Prayer points out the way by consecrating everything we do—our prayers, works, joys, and sufferings—to the all-consuming interest burning in the Sacred Heart. This is a daily offering of our complete self—"a way of life"—a sort of living spirit of love, for love, behind all that we do.

In itself, the day which we offer up to our divine Lord to use for His purpose is of little account. But once He packs it full with His divine life and vitality, it becomes a means of returning our own personal love to Him and an instrument in the sanctification and salvation of others.

The Apostleship of Prayer also teaches us that this constant oneness with our Savior through His divine indwelling is made stronger and more vigorous by our being nourished on the Bread of Life through frequent Holy Communion and a deeper and more ardent love and devotion towards His Mother Mary. There was no one who was more conscious of His divine indwelling than was this woman, the master-piece of all His creations.

So, if you are looking for peace of mind in a world of confusion and have a burning desire to be one with Jesus Christ here on earth and for all eternity in Heaven, listen to these words of Pope Pius XII, who calls devotion to the Sacred Heart of Jesus "the highest act of religion."

Is there a devotion more excellent than that to the Most Sacred Heart of Jesus, one which is more in accord with the real nature of the Catholic Faith or which better meets the needs of the Church and the human race today? What act of religion is nobler, more suitable, sweeter and more conducive to salvation, since this devotion is wholly directed to the love of God Himself?

So if you want to be loved—and we all do—you will find love in all its fullness in the Sacred Heart of Jesus. Your peace, joy and happiness will be found within the shelter of His Loving Heart.

And if you are moved by a lively sense of apostolic action, aflame with the desire of "the Sacred Heart for the world—the world for the Sacred Heart," listen to these words of the Holy Father: "It is also our most ardent desire that all who glory in the name of Christian and who zealously strive to establish the Kingdom of Christ on earth, consider devotion to the Sacred Heart of Jesus as the standard and the source of unity, salvation and peace."

No matter what your walk of life, no matter whether you are old or young, weak or strong, no matter where you live or work or play, you cannot escape the love burning in the Sacred Heart of Jesus. As in past centuries, when that same love fired the hearts of the apostles, confessors, martyrs, and virgins to acts of self-annihilation and heroic courage, so today divine love keeps that same flame leaping forth in all directions to strengthen and warm the hearts of our present-day apostles and teachers of the Word of God—yes, and our own martyrs and confessors, to live and even to die for the love of their Eternal King and Savior, Jesus Christ.

God bless and keep you in His Sacred Heart now and forever.

Just Fifteen Seconds a Day

DID YOU KNOW THAT FIFTEEN SECONDS can change your entire day? You struggle out of bed in the morning and face another eight-hour grind at the office or a monotonous day at the factory. You scramble off to school for another unexciting five hours of grueling exams and lectures. You see nothing glamorous in a washing machine full of soiled diapers or a sink full of dirty dishes. You find the joy of a smiling friendly face so short-lived, the dull hammering pain of a headache—oh, so long-lasting!! But there can be something behind every action and duty, no matter how trivial or boring, that can transform it into something noble and eternally important. Yes, there can be something purposeful in the washer full of diapers—something meaningful in the joys and sorrows, pains and aches, successes and failures of each day.

The difference in your day is the fifteen seconds it takes you to say, the "Morning Offering" prayer. With that daily offering as the purifying element of intention, every prayer, work, joy, and suffering of the day becomes fuel for that blazing furnace of divine love—the Sacred Heart of Jesus! Then your sink is linked to thousands of altars throughout the world; your headache is united with the slow, rotting martyrdom of an imprisoned priest in a concentration camp in China; your joys and successes rise up with the alleluias and hosannas to the Risen Savior; your whole life becomes a continued refrain of adoration, thanksgiving, praise, and reparation to the Creator of the Universe—all for one fifteen-second "Morning Offering" of your day for the same intentions that burn in the Sacred Heart. This daily consecration of self through the Morning Offering prayer is the very essence of the Apostleship of Prayer, and because of it everything is transformed into supernatural value for all eternity. This is not a devotion, but a complete way of life. Through it, all people of every race and color, lay people as well as those in the service of God, participate as hidden dynamos of supernatural power, thus not only sanctifying themselves but overflowing out to those who are near and dear—even to the farthest corners of the world!

Back in the year 1844, at Val, France, a Jesuit priest, Father Francis Xavier Gautrelet, realized the hidden value of this Apostleship of Prayer and inspired the young seminarians preparing for the priesthood and missionary life to be apostles at home, at least in spirit, while still in studies. He suggested that they daily offer up to God their prayers, duties, studies, play, and sacrifices, and through these to beg God's help for the priests and missionaries already in the field and the graces for conversions.

The suggestion caught fire and soon spread to neighboring villages, churches, convents, and other institutions. It wasn't long until the whole country of France and other countries were captivated by this idea of becoming apostles of prayer by this daily consecration of prayers, works, joys, and sufferings. Since then the Apostleship of Prayer has spread throughout the world, until today [1960] it is estimated that there are nearly forty million members, including six million in the United States alone. With it grew also the practice of First Friday Holy Communions of reparation, the devotion of the Holy Hour, the Consecration of the Family, and other devotions to the Sacred Heart.

The tremendous success and secret of this crusade for souls is the fact that in it we are all one in the Mystical Body of which Christ is the Head, and whatever good we do has an effect on the other members. I might liken this spread of sanctity to the chain reaction of a single atom splitting up, and then having an effect on another atom, as it in turn splits up and then another and another, millions of times over, each affecting the other until finally there is a mighty explosion. In the Mystical Body, the impact of the total sanctity of each member is so supernaturally dynamic as to cover the whole face of the earth with the love of God. This is how we become twenty-four-hour-a-day apostles without going to the missions, without preaching sermons. This is the Apostleship of Prayer.

God bless and keep you in His Sacred Heart now and forever.

Mary is My Mother

MARY IS MY MOTHER!

One thought like this can do a great deal to foster a deep abiding love and devotion toward our Blessed Mother—a thought that can unite us as close as the bond between mother and child. Mary is my Mother! Why?

I call Mary my Mother because I know that through the infinite merits of her Son, I have been raised up to a participation in His divine nature. I am reliving the life of Jesus Christ through the life of grace. Truly, then, Mary is my Mother because she beholds her Child in me. I know that by striving habitually for an awareness of the divine indwelling of Jesus Christ in me, I have a sure means of having Mary watch over and protect me as a loving mother. She cannot help but love me because I am her child. Every fiber of her humanity pours out in love for me because of this bond uniting us two by the ties of sanctifying grace.

What a happy doctrine to know that the Mother of God is also our Mother, to know that we can be conscious of the fact that she feels toward us as any mother would toward her child. She is far more than a mother in a figurative sense. Mary is not merely like a mother; she is really our Mother!

Is not a mother one who gives life? And has not Mary given us life—no, not our physical, natural life, but far more important, the infinite, supernatural life of God in our souls—a life which here on earth is already a beginning of the glorious life we shall have in Heaven if we persevere in reliving the life of her Son through grace.

At an awesome moment in history, according to God's plan of redemption, it depended on Mary, on her free consent, whether or not this supernatural life would be imparted to us through our Lord Jesus

Christ. By her free consent, we were reborn to this divine life—raised up to the infinite plane of God Himself. So all-compelling was this tremendous gift that later on in the life of Saint Paul, he could cry out in rapture, "I live, now, not I but Christ lives in me" (Gal 2:20).

True, we are not God, but we have His life in us! We are not God, but we are God's own adopted children! We are not God, but we have the supernatural life of His only begotten Son dwelling in us! What a transforming gift! No wonder Saint John cried out: "And this is the testimony that God has given us, eternal life. And this life is in His Son. He that hath the Son hath life; He that hath not the Son hath not life. These things I write to you that you may know that you have eternal life, you who believe in the name of the Son of God" (1 Jn 5:11–13).

Mary is our Mother, because she has begotten us to this supernatural life of grace. In other words, it is to her, after Jesus Christ, that we are indebted for our supernatural life, this life of the children of God, and for whatever has to do with the production in us of that life, its preservation and development. She is our Mother, as it were, according to the spirit and in the order of grace because she is the Mother of our divine Savior according to the flesh and in the order of nature. It is to this great fact that the Fathers and Doctors of the Church constantly refer us as the basis on which rests the spiritual motherhood of Mary.

The Mother of God is our Mother because she gave her free consent to the mystery of the Incarnation, for the Incarnation looked ahead to the passion and death of Him who would be born of her as the condition of our rebirth. The Son of God became man that we might have His life through His death. That is why in God's divine Providence, Mary's consent was needed and why God left it to her free consent to accept a dignity involving so great a sacrifice. From the moment Mary declared to the angel Gabriel that she accepted her Maker's will, "Behold the handmaid of the Lord, be it done unto me according to thy word" (Lk 1:38), our redemption—our rebirth to the supernatural life—was assured. It was from that moment that we must date her spiritual Motherhood in our regard.

We might add further that there is still something lacking to make that Motherhood toward us complete. She must stand by the cross of Jesus and bring forth her spiritual children in anguish and bitterness of soul. As the Mother of all the living, she must give them spiritual life through the pangs of childbirth as she endures the Passion of her Son. It was on Golgotha that Jesus won for us the grace of divine adoption by the outpouring of His Blood. How very much in order it was then that He should crown His love toward us by making open proclamation to the world that His dearest possession, His own Mother, was to be our Mother. "When Jesus, therefore, saw His Mother and the disciple John standing by whom He loved, then He said to His Mother, 'Woman, behold thy son', and to the disciple he said, 'Behold thy Mother'" (Jn 14:26–27). One has only to read the Gospels and Epistles of Saint John to perceive, as we have seen, how he burned with the love of His divine Master, dwelling in Him. From that moment on, as a son to his Mother, he took Mary to his heart. He was to relive the life of Jesus in his as he watched over and cared for Jesus' Mother.

These words of Christ on the cross were not symbolical only, but effective! For just as He made Saint John the representative of the race of man for whom He suffered and died, so He made His Mother the Mother of all men by her becoming the Mother of the Beloved Disciple. We, her children, are witnesses to the pangs of spiritual childbirth on Calvary, for as Jesus died for all men, the Mother who gave Him to us in turn was given to be our Mother that she might watch over and care for our supernatural upbringing, so that all of us might be made conformable to the image of her Son and continue to relive His life through us.

The thought that my heavenly Mother is God's own masterpiece leaves me utterly bewildered. I know if I had the power to create my mother, I would have made her the most perfect of all creations. But the Son of God had that power! No wonder Saint Bonaventure cried out, "Though God could create a more perfect world, He could not create a more perfect mother than the Mother of God." And this woman is my Mother! What a joy to know that I, therefore, having the most perfect Mother, will always be cared for and protected in a most perfect way from harm. If I start to swerve from the path, she will take me by the hand and lead me back to safety. My relationship to Mary reminds me of the story about the small boy who is crossing the street with his mother. With his hand firmly in hers, he isn't afraid of the dangers. He has complete confidence in his mother leading him to safety. Suddenly he trips, stumbles, and falls. Almost with reproach in his eye he looks up at his mother and cries, "Mommy, why don't you watch where I'm going?"

I, too, am crossing the dangerous road of life in order to reach the other side in safety, but I know with Mary, my Mother, by my side and with her hand in mine I have nothing to fear. If I stumble and fall, she will always be there to lift me up and lead me in safety to the other side. I, with the life of Jesus dwelling in me, cannot fail, for Mary is my Mother!

God bless and keep you in His Sacred Heart now and forever.

4

God is Everywhere

IT WAS AN AWESOME and impressive sight to see our three astronauts on television orbiting about the moon for the first time in the history of the world, but it was still more breathtaking to hear the Word of God coming back to earth when they quoted from the Book of Genesis in the Old Testament. "In the beginning God created heaven and earth . . ."

Truly, how small the earth then appeared to be! Thrown out on the immense sea of the universe, it seemed to be but a tiny pebble among the almost limitless galaxies of millions and millions of stars, all of which God holds in the palm of His hand! And yet, this same God chose our infinitesimally small world to become man and dwell among us! "Why?"—we ask over and over again! And the only answer is that He loves man, His own image, with a passion equal only to the divine—a love that is infinitely beyond our finite minds to comprehend.

When we were asked the question as little children, "Where is God?," the answer came quickly to our lips. "God is everywhere." But how difficult such a simple answer is to comprehend! Has not each one of us wondered just what God in Himself is like—this all-powerful Being who can be everywhere at one and the same time? I know I have! Many years ago, when we were being instructed on how to pray, we were told to place ourselves in the presence of God. But how could we do this? What was God like? Was He some kind of a tremendous Being, a sort of an ever-seeing, long-bearded, benevolent overseer with His arms outstretched over the whole world? Sometimes He is painted in such a manner, but such a picture is a pure figment of the imagination and has no reality whatsoever outside the mind. God in His essence is not human at all. He is divine in nature. But I have to admit that all my mental wrestling brought me little success in trying to imagine the infinite majesty and power of the Almighty upon whom I depend for everything I have and everything I am. I was still unable to feel that real closeness to Him or be aware of His presence in facing the ordinary, prosaic activities of everyday living.

But God Himself solved this problem by relating Himself to man in a visible, tangible, sensible way by becoming man—assuming a human nature exactly like ours with a human soul, mind, and will, like us in everything except sin. Now it was so much easier to put myself in the presence of God through the humanity of Jesus Christ, the Son of God. Now no one could ever say, "God, up in the faraway heavens, or wherever You are, You don't know what crosses I have to carry, what sufferings I have to bear! You don't know what it is to be misunderstood and thought little of—to be a failure and laughed at! You don't know what it is to be a man!" No—for God does know, because He became one of us here in this world! So now to put ourselves in the presence of God is to contemplate our Savior, Jesus Christ, when He was here on earth; hear the words that fell from His blessed lips as He preached words of encouragement and understanding; watch Him as he moved about among the people bringing comfort, strength, and forgiveness to all who came to Him; even feel the warmth of His joyful presence as He repeats to each one of us, "Come to Me, all you who labor and are heavily burdened, and I will refresh you" (Mt 11:20).

Yes, here at last was a powerful way to acquire an awareness of the presence of God. But there was still another way of experiencing His presence, even in a more intimate, personal manner. This would be through His divine indwelling within our souls by the life of grace. By the very fact that He assumed a human nature, He necessarily limited Himself to the narrow confines of Palestine, and the number of people whom He contacted was very limited. Then He died and left this world. Yet He was launching a program for salvation of souls that was to last until the end of time. How was He to accomplish this?

He would do it through other willing humanities. Each one of us would become His other-self in the era of time and the world in which we live. "I have come," He said, "that you may have life, and have it more abundantly" (Jn 10:10). "Abide in Me as I in the Father" (Jn 15:9). And through the life of grace which He merited for us by becoming man, we now have the presence of God—the Blessed Trinity Itself—within our very souls every second of our life here on earth, and this life of union with Him will be consummated in the Beatific Vision through the eons of eternity.

God bless and keep you in His Sacred Heart now and forever.

5

Man, An Extension
of the Blessed Trinity

SOME YEARS AGO, I had the privilege of making a "Better World Retreat" under the direction of Father Ricardo Lombardi, S.J., a renowned preacher and retreat master from Italy. I would like to pass on a few ideas to you.

God in Himself is a community: the Three divine Persons in one divine nature. He willed to extend His community of three Persons to millions of persons like Himself. In His divine plan, He willed to create man after His own image and communicate love, joy, and divine life. Through this divine communication, we become sons of God, our heavenly Father. This first communication of divine life was lost by our first parents, but "happy fault" it was, as Saint Augustine said: "by reason of this fault the heavenly Father, moved by the Holy Spirit of divine love, sent His only-begotten Son, Jesus Christ, to become man." By His becoming man, He would unify man, and all of us would become members of His Mystical Body, lifted up to the life of God Himself.

Jesus Christ is the Son of God by nature; we are the sons of God by adoption. By reason of this adoption we can truly call God "Our Father," and know that He loves each one of us with the same infinite love that He loves His Eternal Son. Adopted children are loved as much as natural children and share equally in the inheritance with them. It follows, then, that we have our divine Savior to be our Brother and share equally with Him as coheirs of the kingdom of Heaven.

A father's thought was in the mind of God, and a father's love in the heart of God when He created me personally. He gave me a share, not only in His being; gave me not only life, but a share in His own divine life, so that I might not be just another creation, but His child—and that forever in the Blessed Trinity.

Everlasting union with the Blessed Trinity is my destination, not by the force of my own nature, but by the divine adoption of my Father in Heaven. No wonder Saint John could exclaim in wonderment, "Behold, what manner of love the Father has bestowed upon us that we should be called the children of God, and such we are" (1 Jn 3:1). Saint Paul, too, over and over again speaks of our divine sonship, as he wrote to the Romans, "You have received a spirit of adoption as sons, by virtue of which we cry, Abba (Father). For the Spirit Himself gives testimony to our spirit that we are the sons of God" (Rom 8:15–16). Saint Peter expressed it in these words, "We are partakers of His divine nature" (2 Pt 1:4). By this participation of course, we are not God, but as His sons, we participate in His divine activity through the gift of sanctifying grace merited by the life and death of Jesus Christ, His Eternal Son. He takes up His life in us through this life of grace, and bilocates Himself through our humanity. Not that we are in any way equal to God, but He, our loving Father, permits us to participate in His divine activity—His supernatural operations through the indwelling of His divine Son. Christ multiplies Himself through this divine indwelling over and over again. Each one of us relives every phase of His life here on earth—His joyful, His sorrowful, and we shall share in His glorious life—and that forever. This is the divine plan of God to extend His community of the Blessed Trinity; this is the consummation of perfect love; this is Heaven.

But we cannot reach this complete oneness with God in Heaven unless we are willing to go all the way with Jesus Christ here on earth. Saint Peter sets an example for us in this regard. Human as he was and frightened at the prospect of dying for Christ during the early persecutions, he was hurrying out of Rome when he met Christ carrying His cross on the way into Rome. When Peter asked Christ where He was going, our divine Lord answered, "Back to Rome, to be crucified again in your place." That was enough for Peter. He turned around, rushed back to Rome to be crucified right there in the Eternal City just like his Master had been in Jerusalem—only upside down. We can almost hear him joyfully exclaiming to his executioners, "I am not worthy to die the way my Master did, but if you must crucify me, crucify me with my head downwards."

Today our divine Lord is speaking to each one of us as He did to Peter—to follow Him all the way in life and in death or into whatever is asked of us, so that in the end we might share with Him the life and love of our Eternal Father and the Holy Spirit for all eternity.

God bless and keep you in His Sacred Heart now and forever.

6

Mirroring the Inner Vision

I REMEMBER as a young child seeing a particular picture in our home which impressed itself so deeply upon my mind that through all these ensuing years, I've never forgotten it. It was a painting of a beautiful woman sitting on top of the world, and at the bottom were penned the words, "The best of everything on earth is you, Jean dearest."

I'll not forget these words, for they were written by my father to my mother, and I know how they welled up from the very depths of his heart and soul and clamored for expression in words of love. I'm sure he recognized in her a reflection, as it were, of the beauty, goodness, sweetness, purity, and loveliness of God Himself, and every vibration of his heart went out to her in love. To him she truly was a mirror of the inner vision of the Creator in whom is all perfection. I only hope and pray that someday I shall share their happiness, for they have both long since gone home to Him.

Isn't it true that love knocks at the gate of the soul and all but bursts the thin wall of the body as it cries out for some kind of external expression of the inner vision of God dwelling there? One might go so far as to say that there would not be a single masterpiece of painting, sculpture, or art in the world if there were not some deep-hidden, powerful love challenging the mind and heart of man to reproduce, as far as humanly possible in external achievement, some of the beauty and perfection of the divine Source of it all. For even though the daring efforts of the artist or the painter or the sculptor fall far short of this inner ire of divine artistry and perfection working within their soul, still a tiny spark of it breaks through to give us the great masterpieces in the world today.

Certainly, anyone who has listened to this voice within their heart must be aware of the manner in which this divine love hurtles over space and time, defies separation and death itself, and announces its encouraging message of everlasting life. For when God chose to create man after His own image and likeness, it was almost as though He took a mirror and seeing a reflection of Himself, breathed into it the breath of life. In beholding man, He cannot help but see Himself, and thus we might say, putting it in human language, every fiber of His infinite truth, goodness, and love goes into His masterpiece of creation.

How consoling it is to realize that because God's love is so great, there is in each of us this same spark of divine indwelling. His love is so intense that He was not content with giving us only natural human life, but a share in His own divine supernatural life. Human by nature, yes, we are now divine by grace—the adopted children of God, the Father; co-heirs with Jesus Christ for the kingdom of Heaven, sacred temples of the Holy Spirit; living tabernacles of the triune God Himself—all because God loves us so much. Now we can go about our everyday duties with the inner consciousness that we're never alone—that our divine Lord Himself uses our humanity to bless our little world wherever we may go or happen to be. Through us radiate the peace and joy of the vision of God's life to all with whom we come in contact.

And for ourselves, an awareness of this great mystery gives us new enthusiasm and courage to be cheerful in the midst of trial and suffering, to be at peace in the throes of temptation and heartache, to keep strong on the royal road of the cross—for now we have the strength of divine life to sustain us.

The words of the beloved disciple, Saint John, "God is love and he who abides in love, abides in God and God in him," (1 Jn 4:16) are emphasized over and over again by Saint Paul and the Fathers of the Church. One most striking example of this is the admonition of Saint Paul to the Corinthians, "Do you not know that your body is a temple of the Holy Spirit within, whom you have from God, and that you are not your own? For you have been purchased at a price. Therefore, glorify God in your body" (1 Cor 6:19-20). Saint Augustine in the fourth century breathed the happy words, "This wonderful union which is properly called indwelling differs only in degree, or state, from that which beautifies the saints in Heaven." In all truth we can say, then, that when our soul is in God's friendship in the state of grace, it is not only the vestibule of Heaven, but the living temple of the Blessed Trinity.

Truly, this is the secret of sanctity—herein lies the power of holiness, for by this divine life we become a mirror reflecting the inner vision of God Himself in a world that needs Him so much.

God bless and keep you in His Sacred Heart now and forever.

7

Explaining Our Faith

IN THE WORLD OF RAPID COMMUNICATIONS, today there is certainly a greater understanding regarding religious faiths among peoples of whatever race or creed everywhere, but even so there are still some false ideas concerning the Catholic Faith. To correct even one of such erroneous notions is of tremendous value. This was never so forcefully brought home to me as on the occasion when I asked a young man whom I had taught for a year if he ever thought of going ahead and learning more about the Catholic Faith. "Oh, I could never be a Catholic," he answered. "Why not?" I asked. His answer shocked me! "Because you Catholics believe that Mary is divine—that she is a goddess, and I could never accept that."

Suffice it to say that I explained in short order that such was not the truth at all, and that if a Catholic worshiped Mary as divine, they would be guilty of serious sin. "She is a creature," I went on to explain, "and in no sense of the word is she, or can she ever be on an equal plane with the Creator. She was created by God and remains on this finite level. Of course, of all God's creations she is His masterpiece because He chose her from all mankind to be His Mother, the channel through whom He would come to earth." I quickly added, "If you had the power of creating your own mother, wouldn't you have made her as perfect as possible? God had that power, and that's exactly what He did—but she is still not divine."

He breathed a sigh of relief with this hurried explanation, almost as though a great burden was lifted from his shoulders. Now he opened up his mind to a clearer explanation of other truths.

I have found this young man's case to be a rather ordinary one, for once the error is dispelled or clarified, the individual can hardly wait to learn more about religion and the basic truths that affect his daily living. It is truly amazing how much interest in the Faith can be generated by clearing up just one little problem. But I would say right here and now that these questions should not be left only to the priests to answer. Everyone should be prepared to answer the common objections and problems that arise, and if he is not so prepared, to be humble enough to admit it and then do a little bit of extra investigation and reading on the subject under discussion.

Strange as it may seem to us, we probably know a great deal more about our Faith than we give ourselves credit for. Of course, we must never forget that the grace of God is always there to be of help, and if we are sincere, what our divine Lord Himself said, "Do not be concerned what you will say—it will be given to you" will work in and through us if we have confidence in Him. We must never give the impression that we are out to snare others or rope them in, but when we ourselves are sincere in our belief and present a convincing example of living Christianity, others cannot help but be drawn to listen to our words and follow our example.

It seems to me that many non-Catholics are kept from the Church by misunderstanding, not the essential doctrines, but matters of secondary importance at best, such as statues, medals, pictures, candles, incense, and other practical means the Church institutes to foster devotion. Actually when the one seeking information about these matters is told that they are simply meant as aids to devotion and are reminders of the spiritual side of life, and that they do not contain any magical powers and are not really necessary at all, most of their difficulties are immediately solved. As far as the saints are concerned, why do we reverence them? It is the same idea as the honor we give to those who are dear to us, or our national heroes who have fought the good fight here on earth, and are now with God in Heaven. God honors His heroes, so why shouldn't we?

Now and then, some people come up with the age-worn objections regarding the compatibility of divine revelation and science. This is easily answered by stating that the Author and Architect of both is the omnipotent God, and there cannot possibly be a conflict or contradiction between them. If there appears to be such, it is definitely a lack of scientific research or a not having a proper and intelligent understanding of what God has revealed. We hold the Bible to be the revealed Word of God, but it must be interpreted in the light of the times during which it was written. It is certainly not a collection of mere pious myths or folklore. Catholics are encouraged to read the Bible daily in a spirit of prayer, learn from it, and be nourished by it.

Other questions also, such as on divorce and remarriage, the Church's stand on birth control and abortion, the Holy Eucharist and confession, and any other pertinent questions can be stated in reasonable, plain terms as to exactly what we believe and hold, not with the idea of convincing the questioner then and there, but of aiding him to better understand our position. In this way we often find that all of us, no matter what Faith or belief we hold, are much closer than we ever imagined. "Good example" is the most eloquent sermon we can ever preach and will do far more towards uniting Christendom than the most persuasive arguments.

God bless and keep you in His Sacred Heart now and forever.

8

Love Calls For Union

HOW TRUE IT IS that when we love someone very much we want to be near the one we love. Such is the love between a devoted husband and wife, or a loving child and his parent, or a young man engaged to the girl of his dreams.

So it is with the greatest man who ever walked this earth—really, greater than man because He was God—Jesus Christ. He came into this world with one burning desire—to be near those whom He loved—to unite Himself with each one of us in a bond so close and intimate that it is like the union between His Eternal Father and Himself. "Holy Father," He prayed for His Apostles at the Last Supper, "keep in Thy Name those whom Thou hast given me, that they may be one even as we are . . . Yet not for those only do I pray, but for those also who through their word are to believe in Me, that all may be one, even as Thou, Father, in Me and I in Thee, that they may be one, even as we are one: I in them and Thou in Me" (Jn 17:11, 20–21, 23).

Isn't this wonderful—the two of us are one—Jesus and I—by means of this divine life which He came into this world to share with man! "I have come that you may have life," He says, "and have it more abundantly" (Jn 10:10). "I am the way, the truth and the life" (Jn 14:6). What an exchange! Jesus Christ is the bridge between the infinite and the finite—linking humanity to divinity—and thus lifting men up to a participation in the supernatural life of God Himself.

This union between Christ and myself is so necessary in order to preserve this divine life dwelling in me that if I be separated from Him for one instant I will wither away and die. "I am the vine and you are the branches," He warns; "He who abides in Me, and I in him, he bears much fruit; for without Me you can do nothing" (Jn 15:5). "As the Father has loved Me, I also have loved you. Abide in My love" (Jn 15:9–10). No wonder each of us should pray from the depths of our soul, "Oh divine Savior, permit me never to be separated from Thee!"

Saint Paul was so overpowered by the necessity of keeping this living union between Christ and himself that he cried out, "I am sure that neither death, nor life, nor angels, nor principalities, nor things present, nor things to come, nor powers, nor height, nor depth, nor any other creature will be able to separate us from the love of God which is in Christ Jesus our Lord" (Rom 8:38–39). He spoke as though Christ Himself were speaking through him, "With Christ I am nailed to the cross. I live, now not I, but Christ lives in me" (Gal 2:19–20).

Later, Paul proved in action how convinced he was of the power and strength of Christ's divine life flowing through him. He was preaching to the early Christians in the town of Troas. Carried away by his burning zeal to spread the love of Christ among his listeners and to explain this living union between Christ and those who love him through sanctifying grace and the reception of Holy Communion, he forgot time and went on until midnight.

Saint Luke narrates in the Acts of the Apostles that "a certain young man named Eutychus, who was sitting on the windowsill, was sinking into a deep sleep as Paul talked on and on. Once overcome by sleep, he fell down from the third story and when he was picked up, he was dead. Paul went down, threw himself upon him, and said as he embraced him, 'Don't be alarmed; there is life in him'" (Acts 20:9–10). The great Apostle—practicing what he preached, not in the least shaken by the incident—standing up in their midst and raising his hands over the people in silent prayer for a moment must have reassured them that there was nothing to worry about, that he could do all things in Him Who strengthened him. The next moment that boy who had been dead got up alive with vital blood coursing through his veins once again.

Who performed that stupendous miracle? Was it Paul? No, for no man has power over life and death! It was Jesus Christ Himself dwelling in him, using His ambassador as a willing instrument to prove that the lesson He was teaching of His divine indwelling in those who love God and obey His Commandments is true.

This brings to mind the little boy who was on his deathbed and the priest asked him the question, "Son, are you afraid to die?"

"Afraid to die? No, I'm not afraid to die."

"And why aren't you afraid?," the priest persisted.

"Because I want to go where Jesus is."

"But what if Jesus goes to Hell?"

With a smile on his lips, the dying boy answered, "Where Jesus is, there is no Hell."

How true! What a consoling doctrine this is, to know that we are never alone, that Christ is always with us no matter where we are or where we go, that in Him, we have the way, the truth, and the life—and there is nothing that we two, working together as one, cannot accomplish here in time and for all eternity.

God bless and keep you in His Sacred Heart now and forever.

9

The Apostleship of Prayer

THE STORY IS TOLD of a chambermaid in England who, while making one of the beds in an old castle, heard the sound of something falling from under the bed onto the floor. Getting down on her hands and knees to see what it was, she was delighted to find that it was a gold coin. Excitedly, she ran to the master of the house and told him the story. What do you think they discovered upon investigation when they returned to the bed? Of course they turned everything upside down, and there under the ancient springs was a false bottom with a hidden compartment, which contained a treasure of silver and gold and precious jewels of inestimable value.

Now wouldn't it be wonderful if every time you made your bed in the morning you found a golden coin? Wouldn't it be a pleasant surprise if every time you washed a dish, there before your startled eyes would sparkle a lustrous diamond? Every time you picked up your pen at the office or your hammer in the workshop, there on your desk or bench you would discover a treasure—a jewel or a coin—of great value.

Ordinarily such a course of events will not take place in a material way, but in another sense, spiritually speaking, when we have the divine Life of Christ dwelling within our souls through sanctifying grace, by purity of intention through the Morning Offering, we are accumulating a wealth that is of much more value—and that for all eternity! This is the very essence of the Apostleship of Prayer—to make everything count supernaturally so that in all our daily actions—prayers, sufferings, joys—we find a treasure of infinite, everlasting value. It is so simple!

Actually it is living, as it were, a consecrated life of daily dedication in union with our divine Savior. Stated simply, it is the reliving of the life of Christ in ours through grace. He lets us share the fruits of His redemptive act and continue to carry out His mission of saving souls through our humanity.

By the very human nature that He assumed, He necessarily limited Himself to the narrow confines of Palestine and to the particular age in which He lived. Actually, He willed to save the souls of all men in every age until the end of time. How was He going to bring this about?

Here is the answer: through this divine life of grace which he merited for us by living His life here on earth and dying on the cross, He would multiply Himself over and over again in other willing humanities until the end of time. Each one of us, so human by nature, becomes a divine participant by grace, and through us, our divine Savior is able to continue His apostolate in the world today. Through sanctifying grace we are constantly reliving some phase of His life in ours when we unite everything we do—our joys, prayers, sufferings, works, and all things else—with His joys, prayers, works, and sufferings; and He ennobles, sanctifies, lifts them up to His supernatural, infinitely meritorious level.

This Apostleship of Prayer permeates our every breathing moment, even when we are asleep—for we have the divine life of Christ in us, and we are uniting everything with Him through our daily Morning Offering. Through this wonderful life of grace, we today, in the age in which we live, can make up for what was wanting in the Passion of Christ, even though it took place centuries ago.

Recently I was at the hospital bedside of a woman who had just undergone a severe throat operation that very morning. She was suffering excruciating pain, and I knew her nerves were stretched to the utmost limit of endurance when the other occupants of her room began to talk in loud voices and made jarring unnecessary noises. In sympathy I told her how my heart went out to her, hoping that things would soon quiet down for her sake. She couldn't talk, but taking a piece of paper she wrote, "It wasn't quiet for Jesus on the cross either."

Truly this good woman had the correct idea of uniting her suffering with Christ on the cross. No, it wasn't quiet on Calvary that first Good Friday afternoon—what with all the shouts and jeers, hoots and blasphemies heaped upon our dying Savior! This is the way we make up for what was wanting in the Passion of Christ, for when He hung on the cross on Calvary centuries ago, all was present to Him. He saw each one of us and how much we would be willing to unite ourselves daily with Him—to make our joys, His joys; our works, His works; our prayers, His prayers; our sufferings, His sufferings.

Through this marvelous Apostleship of Prayer, we now continue His life here in the world today by sanctifying all that we do or think and say—and only in eternity will we behold the treasure we have accumulated which neither the rust will destroy nor the moths consume.

So all you shut-ins, you bedridden sufferers, you busy housewives, you hard working fathers, you growing children, take consolation. You are doing wonderful work for God—you are the true Apostles of Prayer saving souls. Sanctify your day—sanctify your work, your joys, your pains and sufferings. Only the living God in Heaven knows the number of those who are there because of you. Some day you will know when they greet you with a smile and say, "Thank you, dear friend; our Loving Savior, Jesus Christ, has brought me here through you."

God bless and keep you in His Sacred Heart now and forever.

10

The Lay Apostolate

DID YOU EVER STOP TO THINK that it is within the power of each one of us to be a vital instrument in God's hands to bring about the eternal salvation of souls? It is evident that in this most important campaign, the priests, sisters, and brothers, those especially consecrated to God, cannot do it all alone. He has united all in His Mystical Body, the lay people as well as the religious, as one in the bond of love and invites everyone in all states of life to be His active helpers in building up a better world, both in time and eternity.

Such a supernatural charity and responsibility towards our neighbor is of the very essence of the lay apostolate. Try as we might we cannot escape this responsibility, for whether we realize it or not, we all exert an influence, either for good or bad, on those around us. By the very fact of our incorporation in Christ through baptism, we must be willing to give of ourselves generously and self-sacrificingly, and to the utmost degree of our talents in influencing others towards Christ and all He stands for.

How many golden opportunities there are to put this into practice! I can't help but think of the young nurse friend of mine at a non-sectarian hospital in California who had this responsibility ever before her, and at every opportunity put it into practice. On one occasion I was visiting a patient there and happened by mere chance to run into this particular nurse who told me of a deaf man who was dying in her ward. Knowing how to use the sign language from my work with these unfortunate handicapped people, I hurried up to see him. Because of their inability to converse, those who were taking care of him weren't sure if he was mentally alert, but when I asked him his name in signs and he spelled out both his first and last name, I was pretty sure he was sufficiently alert to go on. So I told him how happy I was to see him and asked if he believed in God. He answered that he did. Then I continued in the sign language asking if he believed in God the Father, and Jesus Christ, His Son, who became man and died on the cross for us, and in the Holy Spirit. As far as I could judge, he answered "yes" to all these questions.

But when he signed after me, "I love you, Jesus Christ," I knew he was ready. I was convinced, so I signed, "Do you wish to be baptized?" He shook his head, "yes." The nurse gave me a cotton pad with water. Then I squeezed the water onto his head, saying the words of baptism, "I baptize you in the Name of the Father and of the Son and of the Holy Spirit." Then when he signed that he was sorry if he had ever offended God, I gave him conditional absolution, in case he had already been baptized before. What blessings came upon him that day! I placed a Sacred Heart badge and a happy death crucifix to his lips, and he kissed them both very fervently and devoutly. I knew he was ready to die and face his Judge, Jesus Christ.

Here is a perfect example of divine Providence—that I should happen to be there at the hospital that day and be one of the few priests who could make use of the sign language to help this suffering man die in peace. It was a great consolation to me, but at the same time I knew it wasn't through anything I had done myself. It's true I was our divine Lord's ambassador, taking His place—but that little nurse had been the means, the lay apostle, who recognized an opportunity to save a soul and made use of it. I learned later that the deaf man died not long after my visit. How the angels must have rejoiced to present the beautiful tapestry of his soul before the court of Heaven!

And there were so many others praying behind the scenes and suffering in union with Christ on the cross—offering everything up to Him for the intentions burning in His Sacred Heart. Such as these were doing the real soul-saving work—hidden dynamos of prayer and pain. They were the true apostles bringing souls to heaven.

It takes only a moment for a bullet to pierce your heart in martyrdom for Christ, but sometimes the daily grind of a living martyrdom for His sake is a great deal harder than dying for Him. But the important and consoling thing to remember is that by living a Christ-like life you are truly His apostle—saving souls. Even though you may never preach a sermon or baptize one single soul, you are a hidden leaven of goodness or a silent rebuke to those who would compromise with their conscience as they throw aside the goodness and purity, truth and honesty of Jesus Christ.

Each one of us needs to put Christ so much into his life that wherever he is or goes—at home or in the field, in school or at the ball game, in the office or at the workshop—he will bring Christ, radiate Christ, breathe Christ, live Christ. Such is the lay apostle, a fit tool in the hand of God for the salvation of his neighbor on earth and a constant delight to the Heart of God in Heaven.

God bless and keep you in His Sacred Heart now and forever.

11

Prayer—The Breadth of Our Spiritual Life

IS PRAYER A MATTER OF GREAT DIFFICULTY FOR the average person? No, not if we understand what it means to pray. Basically, it is a conversation with God—thinking out loud and talking things over with the Father, Son, and Holy Spirit. After all, speech is our main means of communicating with one another. So, praying or talking to God is the most natural way to pray.

Some may ask, well, what do you talk to God about? The answer is—just about anything you want to: your children or husband or wife or parents or home life; perhaps your work at the plant, your difficulty in getting along with that fellow who works at your side; your school work or sports; why, even your happy hours, parties, and joyous gatherings; your golf game or knitting; or your worries and plans for the future. God listens to everything.

Gradually you feel more at ease in His presence and listen to Him in the silence of your own heart. As a matter of fact, turning to God within your own self by His divine indwelling makes prayer a constant union with Him in everything you do or think or say. It seems to me that the best way to pray is to invite our divine Lord to take over your humanity and have Him completely captivate you in your daily living. In this way you are never alone, no matter where you go or what you are doing.

I remember one day driving my car and asking Christ to "take over" my humanity and drive the car through me. You see, He never had the joy of driving a high-powered automobile in His day. Do you know what happened? We went right through a boulevard stop!

I like to imagine a conversation with Jesus something like this, "Dear Lord," I said to Him, "do you know what you just did?" And He replied, "No—What's the matter?" "You went right through a boulevard stop," I explained. "For Heaven's sake," was His exclamation (well, that didn't sound bad at all coming from His lips), "I didn't realize what I was doing. You see when I was here on earth all we rode were horses, mules, wagons, and buggies."

Even though I really didn't blame Him for what I had done, to my way of thinking this was truly praying—and it was fun. I like to think of this way of praying as giving a vacation to our Lord in the 20th century. Let Him enjoy seeing things of today's world through your eyes, taking trips through you in an automobile, on an airplane or ocean steamer, or whatever it may be. You see He never had the opportunity in His own humanity to do these things—so why not let Him borrow yours? This is real prayer, believe me.

Actually you don't have to go outside yourself to pray, but just turn inside, knowing that our divine Lord has taken possession of you by His divine indwelling, and He will listen. This kind of prayer is a spontaneous, simple, free sort of loving familiarity with Christ, and I'm sure He too must delight in it.

It's true, vocal or memorized prayers have their place and can assist us at times when we feel sort of far away from God, but they cannot take the place of prayer from the heart, for all of us need this naturalness and freedom with God just as we do with one another. Even to reap the full benefit from the prayers of the liturgy or the rosary or other formal prayers, we must put our heart into them and really make them mean to us from our inner self what they express.

To pray may be difficult at times, but to become proficient in it, like anything else, we must practice it over and over again until it becomes almost like a reflex. But time will take care of our difficulties, and soon our prayer life will blossom like a flower in the morning sun from the deepest recesses of our heart. We must not give up too quickly, for regardless of how distant God may seem to be, He remains closer to you than you are to yourself. Just tell Him how you feel and how cold and dry you are. He will sympathize with you and accept this kind of prayer even more than one where tears flow and you feel His presence very intimately. Always remember that he prays best who is so close to God that he doesn't know he's praying.

Yes, truly, prayer is the breath of our spiritual life—the gentle rising of our heart toward the God who loves us beyond our faintest conception and who listens with joy as we say, "Dear God, I love you."

God bless and keep you in His Sacred Heart now and forever.

12

You, Too,
Have Work to Do

IN THE DIVINE PLAN OF GOD for the salvation of souls, it is not so important what we do, but why we do it. It is the intention and motivation that really counts in the eyes of God and in the light of eternity. It is for this reason that we can say in all truth that those who are sick or crippled or so-called "shut-ins" have work to do, perhaps more than anyone realizes. Only in heaven will the entire truth be known, when those who are in the Beatific Vision with God forever will understand who the soul-savers on earth really were.

When we are sick and tied to our bed, unable to move and do all we would like to do, then we can remember that this is all part of God's plan for the salvation of souls. If He had thought of a better way, He Himself would not have climbed up the hill of Calvary and died on the cross. I am sure at that time He would like to have gone out among the maimed and paralytic and reached out His hand to cure them, but He couldn't because those hands were nailed to the cross. I'm sure He yearned to rush to the side of those who needed His blessing, but He couldn't because His feet were nailed to the cross. So those who are sick and unable to accomplish much externally are reliving this suffering phase of Christ's life in theirs and are truly instruments in His hands in the work of sanctification and salvation of others.

Far from just vegetating during such periods of illness, we can add real zest to our lives by alerting ourselves to the fact that we've got work to do for Christ every second of our day. Take the example of Saint Ignatius of Loyola, a man of action and a soldier in the army of his king. When he was wounded in the leg while fighting in a battle, he became a "shut-in," but it was during this time that a complete transformation came over him. He asked for some romantic novels to while away the time, but none were available. Printed books were so scarce in those days that only two books were found. One of these happened to be a copy of the lives of the saints. He read it and was deeply stirred by the heroism of other men like himself, who were willing to do so much for God at cost to self. He asked himself the question, "These men were of the same frame as I. They were just mortal beings like myself, with all the same stings of passion to overcome. Then cannot I do what they have done?"

As a result of this grace, Ignatius threw himself down on the floor and pledged his allegiance to His divine King, the only one worth living for, worth fighting for, worth dying for. And today there are more than thirty thousand followers of Ignatius banded under his standard of Christ the King, all because Saint Ignatius was forced to be a "shut-in" for a sufficient time to allow the grace of God to work in his soul, and because he cooperated with it. Think of the millions of souls that have been helped and sanctified by the thousands of Jesuits during these past four hundred years since Ignatius decided to go all out for God. Far from looking upon his injury as an excuse to be forlorn and feel sorry for himself, he read, and out of what was an apparently evil thing, good came. Ignatius journeyed to Manresa near the city of Barcelona, and there he went into a retreat for almost a year. From this flowered the Spiritual Exercises that have nourished and given courage to countless men and women to reach the heights of sanctity.

Always remember there is a silver lining to every dark cloud, if only we look for it. You sick and suffering friends of Christ, you are not on the scrap heap. Your life has not ended simply because you are sick—it is just beginning. You can turn your sickness into the most profitable time of your whole life. You, like Ignatius, can turn it into a means of sanctifying yourself, and at the same time you can be an instrument in helping to save the souls of others. You have your mission in this life, and you are not created by God for naught. God has a definite purpose in permitting you to feel desolate, but always remember He Knows what He is doing, and it's all for the best in the light of eternity.

Our Savior, Jesus Christ, teaches us that we are all members of the same Mystical Body of which He is the head. The vitality and health of the whole body depends on the health of all the cells that go to make up that body. The blessing of sickness is that only the physical cells are sick, not the supernatural ones. They are alive and vibrant. Your work is to help the sick and dying cells of those who are in need. You have the power also to shorten the suffering of the souls in Purgatory. I ask you—can there possibly be a greater work that you could do?

There are so many people in the world who need your prayers and help: the Holy Father, our bishop, priests, government leaders, our separated brethren, the dying are all reaching out their hands to you. Will you turn them away sad, or will you offer up your suffering for them? Oh, there are so many things you can pray for! Think of the racial injustice and violence! You can help to bring about a better understanding among all peoples. And godless communism—you can even be an instrument in thwarting this diabolical plan to enslave mankind.

Begin each day with your offering of everything you do or think or say for the intentions of the Sacred Heart, and by so doing you are continuing Christ's work here on earth—the sanctification and salvation of souls. Let me assure you right now—you are needed, for you are fulfilling a most important part of our Savior's work by this daily consecration of yourself to Him.

And so I congratulate all of you wonderful sufferers and bedridden patients, and thank you for helping me personally in my priestly work. You are doing the real soul-saving, believe me. In this light, suffering is not a curse; it is a beautiful blessing from the Heart of Christ Himself.

God bless and keep you in His Sacred Heart now and forever.

13

The Secret of Peace

WHAT IS THE SECRET OF PEACE? This is a question that has been asked millions of times over since time immemorial. What is the secret of peace?

Let me tell you how I would answer that question, and I am speaking specifically of peace of soul. I believe the secret of peace may be expressed in one word—and that word is "Love." When I am conscious of the fact that God loves me personally, and as an individual so much that He Himself is not only satisfied with giving me my ordinary human life, but a share in His own divine life, I cannot help but have a deep inner peace within myself that no power on earth can ever take away from me. This is the kind of peace that the world cannot give and the world cannot take away. When everything is all right between myself and God, and I know He loves me and I am prepared to face Him in judgement, then I am at peace.

After all, what is there to life but this close, most intimate friendship with Jesus Christ, whom I shall possess for all eternity. All other human loves flicker and go out along the highway of life, but His love will endure forever. Every tombstone tells us the same story, as cemetery dust waves requiem over the purest, most noble friendships here on earth. Only His love remains beneath the passing shadows. Thomas à Kempis in his Imitation of Christ summarizes it very well, "Without a friend thou canst not live well, and if Jesus be not your friend above all, thou wilt indeed be sad and desolate."

This is the secret of our peace of soul in the midst of the turmoil and clamor of our earthly existence. No other love will completely satisfy the yearning of our mind and heart and will for truth, good, and love—all of which can only be found in the Source of it all, the

God who created us to share everything that He Himself possesses.

Here on earth, we have a foretaste of what God has in store for those who love Him in the possession of His divine life within our souls. We are never alone any longer, now that we have our dearest Friend always near—in fact, within our very being.

When we were young Jesuits, our Master of Novices used to say, "When you begin to pray, put yourself in the presence of God." At that time I wondered how to go about doing this. Should I imagine God as an all-powerful Person with a long, grey beard, sort of watching over everything from afar, as it were? I had seen pictures on canvas of God the Father portrayed something like this. Or perhaps I should imagine myself taking a walk with Jesus Christ, the Son of God, who took upon Himself the same human nature that I have. Arm-in-arm, then, I could talk things over as with a good friend in whom I could confide and feel perfectly at home. Yes, that was one way of praying and using my imagination and certainly would bring God much closer to me.

But then as the years rushed by and I became more and more aware of His divine indwelling within my very being and that He loves me personally so much that He is present within my whole self, body as well as soul, I realized that to put myself in God's presence was simply a matter of turning my thoughts within myself and letting Him speak and act through me. I think this is what Saint Paul meant when ecstatically he cried out, "I live, now not I, but Christ lives in me" (Gal 2:20).

Truly this is the secret of peace; this is the secret of happiness—the oneness with Christ through the supernatural life of sanctifying grace in the soul. Through the all-vivifying principle of divine life, one cannot help but strive to be more and more like Christ, the divine exemplar and model of perfect human living. I like to call this way of life the "Human Adventure of Divine Living"!

Of course, to achieve this oneness with Christ demands a constant getting rid of self: otherwise there can be no permanent peace. We are somewhat like a donkey that is ashamed of its tail and tries to get rid of it by running away from it. But the more frantic he becomes in running away, jumping here and there, the more persistently the tail follows after. Self-love is like the tail. As long as we remain the selfish donkey, it will follow us wherever we go, but the moment we stop being the donkey by getting rid of self and let Christ "take over" without any hindrance on our part, then Christ will transform us into Himself and there will be peace.

Our daily prayer should be, "Dear Lord, my God and dearest Friend, take possession of my complete self. If You live in me without any interference on my part, then through me You will continue to radiate Your pure and infinite love to Your Father in Heaven, and I will have your strength and courage to live my life for You here on earth."

God bless and keep you in His Sacred Heart now and forever.

14

How to Be a
Spiritual Millionaire

WOULD YOU LIKE TO BE A MILLIONAIRE? Would you enjoy making a fortune that would outlast your lifetime? How about putting some of that kind of currency into the bank that will buy a kingdom of splendor and beauty and will never be destroyed?

I can hear you say, "You bet I would! But how do you go about it? Where's the money coming from? Who's the banker? And what kind of a kingdom are you talking about?"

Let me put it this way. Did you know that you have a spiritual dynamo at your disposal? Are you aware of the fact that you can be spreading the kingdom of Christ, saving souls, and at the same time, be acquiring supernatural virtues and thus building up an imperishable fortune for yourself while watching a good movie or TV program, playing a game, washing dishes or doing your job? Rather amazing, isn't it?

All you have to do is throw the switch which turns on the current and get the motor running. The motor is your soul; the current is the supernatural life of God dwelling in that soul; the power is sanctifying grace; the Morning Offering you say at the beginning of the day is that switch which turns on the motor; and Holy Communion keeps it running smoothly and increases your power. You can be sure with all of this in good operating condition, God the Banker daily stores up your spiritual millions in the eternal vault of Heaven.

Before baptism, you were still down on the natural plane, like an airplane which hasn't its propellers or jet prepared for action. But the moment those waters were poured on your head and the words of baptism said, you took off from this natural plane faster than lightning, broke through the earth's sound barrier, and jetted high up beyond the Milky Way, even beyond the farthest star in the heavens, to the supernatural plane. You became a Superman, as it were, for you became supernaturalized and a child of God Himself. With the coming of sanctifying grace in your soul, you became a temple of the Holy Spirit and have the indwelling of Jesus Christ in you.

As you grew up and were able to think and choose things, either good or bad, you had the power within you to turn on that switch by an act of your free will. In other words, you could deliberately choose to see God in all things. You could supernaturalize your complete day by doing all for Him.

And because by sanctifying grace you have this infinite life of Jesus dwelling in you, your Morning Offering is the same as though Jesus Christ, the Son of God, were saying to His Father through your humanity: "Here, Eternal Father, is my daily offering; take it."

In other words, by keeping yourself in God's love and purifying your intention daily by the Morning Offering, you acquire supernatural virtues here on earth and make everything count for eternity. You become an apostle for the salvation of souls, and at the same time you are building a beautiful castle in the kingdom of Heaven.

This is the life of constant union with God. This is why I say, every moment is a prayer, every breath, every word, every gesture, every step—everything. It is as though we were saying to our divine Master: "Jesus, I know that I am not very much of myself, but with your life dwelling in me, I have all power. Take my daily offering, my body with all its senses and my soul with all its faculties, but above all, take my heart. My little offering in itself is so small—I'm so finite—but with you acting in and through me, my offering becomes infinite in value."

By living our lives in this manner—looking at all things through the eyes of Christ—we cannot help but acquire fixed habits of Christian conduct: humility, meekness, patience, kindness, helpfulness, charity in thought, word, and deed, fidelity, truthfulness, forgiveness of injuries, love of enemies; because it will be He working and praying, acting and living through us. We let Him borrow our humanity that He may multiply Himself millions of times over in the world that needs Him so much today.

God bless and keep you in His Sacred Heart now and forever.

15

Breaking Through the Infinite Sound Barrier

WHEN OUR DIVINE LORD SAID, "I have come to set the earth on fire, and how I wish it were already blazing" (Lk 12:49), He wanted us to know how all-consuming is His desire to spread His burning love and divine life in the hearts and souls of men everywhere. The one purpose of His becoming man, living here on earth, and dying on the cross was the salvation of souls and of each soul in particular. Sometimes we falsely imagine ourselves to be thrown out, as it were, on the great sea of humanity, and we cry out, "How can I be of any importance in God's eyes? Why, I don't amount to very much at all. Look at the millions of people in the world!"

Yet, each one of us is of infinite importance to our divine Savior! I might go so far as to say that if you, as an individual, were the only one in the world, He would not love you more than He does at this very instant.

He is personally interested, not just in people and their salvation in a general way, but in the individual person—you! He manifests that type of love in a special way in the sacrament of the Holy Eucharist. When we receive Him in Holy Communion, does he divide Himself up and say, "All right now, Mary, you can have this part of me, and you, John, this other part." No! To each one individually, He gives Himself completely, body and soul and divinity.

From this we can readily understand how He is vitally concerned about the personal needs and intentions of each one in particular, and everything that has a bearing on his welfare and happiness—his family, friends, children, job, health, vocation, financial matters, worries, anxieties over national and international problems. The list could go on endlessly, but Christ is interested personally in everything that concerns us, no matter how trivial. Our intentions are His intentions.

So, when we pray for the intentions of one another—for the millions of associates, members of the Apostleship of Prayer throughout the world—we join our prayers with those of Christ, and He gives them divine, infinite power. Like His, then, our prayers and works embrace everyone—the pope, bishops, missionaries, rulers of nations, the sick and dying, even sinners and atheists—and bring the needs of each to the attention of our loving Father as we daily storm the battlefront of Heaven for each and every one.

But, you may retort in all sincerity, "What possible effect can my measly prayers and humdrum activities have in influencing the lives and possible salvation of others?"

The answer is simple. Those so-called measly prayers and humdrum activities of yours are now linked through grace to the infinite, supernatural, divine life which Jesus Christ merited for you and as a result are shot through with His divine power and efficacy.

We know, too, how in the Mystical Body of Christ, the Church, we are all one with Christ, the head. Just as in our own physical body one part affects the other, so in the Mystical Body each one of us plays a part on the other. When I, for example, have an infection in my ear, my whole body feels miserable, and when the diseased organ is cured, I feel better all over. This is the way it is in the Mystical Body, also. Each living member in sanctifying grace helps the other members by this daily consecration of prayers, works, joys, and offerings for the intentions of the Sacred Heart. He prays in the Name of Jesus Christ, and thus shares in His divine, supernatural power.

And, we must also remember that this daily offering is not limited just to members of the Catholic Church but is extended to everyone, for Christ wills the salvation of all men of whatever race, creed, or color.

I would add here that those who are nearest and dearest to us are the most affected by our union with Christian prayer. By our own personal sanctification, the fire of His divine life and love will overflow and sanctify our children, our parents, relatives, and dearest friends. Moreover, there is no finite barrier to keep our prayers from leaping over mountains, flying over oceans, and giving power to the missionaries, priests, sisters, and lay mission helpers laboring away from home among those others for whom Christ died.

Right at this very moment while you are reading this talk, a man may be dying, crushed beneath the broken wheels of an automobile during an accident, and because of your offering this morning, you merited for him the grace to elicit an act of perfect love and thus save his soul. We shall never know until eternity the virtue of charity that we practiced towards our fellowmen by this simple formula of daily prayer in union with Christ.

While powerful nations of the world are storing stockpiles of atomic bombs to lay waste the earth with material fire, we are mobilizing spiritual weapons of united prayer to enkindle the fires of divine love in the hearts of men. We have all seen pictures of the frightful mushroom cloud of a nuclear atomic explosion ascending to the outer stratosphere and are aware of the inevitable deadly fallout killing life here on earth. We, too, as tiny atoms are united together working on one another in a mighty explosion of prayer that rises like a mushroom cloud, not just to the outer stratosphere of the earth, but up to the limitless eternity of Heaven—up, up, to the Heart of God Himself. From that pierced Heart there falls, not death-dealing gases of earthly fire, destroying life, but life-giving graces of heavenly fire giving divine life and love to all who will receive them.

God bless and keep you in His Sacred Heart now and forever.

16

The Layperson Today

DOES THE LAYPERSON TODAY play a vital role in the life drama of a person's spiritual development and sanctification here on earth? Is he important and necessary in effecting the salvation of souls for an eternal happiness with God in Heaven? At times, the lay person living in the midst of his worldly and temporal pursuits may think that this type of function should be left entirely to those who are dedicated to God in the priesthood or religious life. But this is not true.

According to God's divine providence, He wills that men be saved through men. In other words, even though He could have accomplished this alone by becoming man and redeeming him by the outpouring of His Precious Blood on the cross of Calvary, He allows men to participate in this redeeming gesture by giving them a share in His own divine life, by grace. By the very fact that He assumed human nature, a body and soul like ours, He necessarily limited Himself to the narrow confines of Palestine and to the era of time in which he lived. And the number of people He contacted directly and personally was relatively few. Yet He was launching a program which would affect the lives of millions until the end of the world. How was He going to bring this about?

He would do this by multiplying Himself through other willing humanities by the gift of sanctifying grace which He merited for them. In other words, He would let men participate in His divine life and be His "other self," as it were, through all the ages to come and in every part of the world. "I will be with you always," He said, "even to the end of the world" (Mt 28:20). "I am the vine; you are the branches" (Jn 15:5). As long as men, the branches, are connected with the vine, Christ, they will relive His life in theirs and continue His salvific work here on earth. It matters little what state of life a person happens to be in, or what type of work he is involved in, as long as he is alive with the life of Christ, he is an effective instrument in His hands for the continual sanctification and salvation of souls. Like Saint Paul, he becomes "another Christ" in the world in which he lives.

The individual layperson may be called upon to be an apostle of Christ in an active way, such as by taking part in the spiritual works of his parish: a Confraternity of Christian Doctrine teacher or promoter of the Sacred Heart, a member of the Christian Family Movement, the Sodality or Legion of Mary, or in any of the many other charitable and social works of the Church in its extensive program to spread Christ's message to all. Because of poor health or some other reason, he may be unable to take an active part in any of these good works. Yet at the same time, he can be just as truly an apostle for good, a missionary for Christ and play as predominant a role in this great work of saving souls as the other fellow, perhaps even more. It's not so important what a person does in the eyes of God, but why he does it that counts in the light of eternity. The good holy layperson, whether he be well or sick, old or young, a college graduate or an unlettered worker in the fields, married or single, by offering up his prayer, works, joys, and sufferings every morning for the intentions of the Sacred Heart, is truly an apostle of prayer reliving Christ's mystical humanity in the world today.

I knew a very devout Catholic layman who I'm sure probably brought about more real, lasting, supernatural good in his life on a bed of pain for almost sixteen years than if he had been well and able to get around. Dr. John J. McDevitt had been an outstanding obstetrician in Los Angeles, California, before he was suddenly struck down with an illness that left him paralyzed on the right side. At first he could hardly form even a word to express his thoughts and desires. And during the last six years of his life, due to lack of circulation gangrene set in his one good leg, necessitating its amputation, which left him completely bedridden.

Perhaps I should tell you a little about this man of God. When he was well, he told me how much he would like to walk down the halls of the hospital and go into the rooms of the sick and stretch out his hand like Christ, touch their wounds, and they would be made well. Now, he couldn't even administer to them and alleviate their pain because like Christ's, his hands and feet were nailed to his cross, the bed on which he lay. Once I saw him, weary and eyes red from lack of sleep, sitting on a stool outside the operating room where he had spent hours in surgery at the side of a woman in danger of bleeding to death from hemorrhages. Some thirty pints of blood had already been transfused into her veins to keep her alive. At that time he showed me the crucifix which he always wore hanging from a chain about his neck and said, "I looked at Christ on the cross and asked Him for help, and thank God, I found the bleeder immediately." The woman delivered triplets who would not be alive today if it hadn't been for the tender care and prayerful courage of that outstanding doctor, who modeled his own life after that of the Divine Physician.

And that's the way it always was with this wonderful man of God— a man of action, yes, but at the same time a man of prayer and confidence in God's help. He had the Christlike combination of projecting himself out to the needs of others with a delicate combination of tenderness and firmness, kindness and utter self-sacrifice. To my way of thinking he was truly a man—ever about his Father's business, whether it was at the operating table or counselling young people in preparation for marriage, or helping them with their marital problems afterwards. He lived his state of life as father and husband modeled on that of the Holy Family at Nazareth—and in so doing was a willing instrument in the hands of Christ for the salvation of souls in this world of today.

When tragedy struck, his outlook—or uplook, I should say—remained ever the same. God's glory and the salvation of souls were uppermost in his mind. Incapacitated through the years, hurting and wasting away in pain, he had a smile for everyone and was always interested in others and their problems, trusting the Sacred Heart, confident that God would take care of him and his family.

After several months of agonizing pain from cancer of the lung, the good doctor died the way he lived. One of his sons lifted the oxygen mask so his father might kiss the crucifix, and amazingly the tired lips, which hadn't moved for hours, formed that kiss. "I love you, Jesus," his wife, Mary, whispered the word into his ear. Then to make sure he understood, she said, "Kiss it again, Jack." And his lips once again closed on the crucifix. (I myself had blessed that same crucifix, and it had the special happy-death blessing attached to it.)

Then the crucifix with a Sacred Heart Badge pinned to it was gently laid in his one good hand, the left one, which now was blue and icy cold. I had tried to get a pulse beat there earlier, but to no avail. Now there was just one more thing he must do. Slowly, with his arm which had been lifeless and still for hours, he lifted the crucifix as high as his heart, and at that moment he quietly took his last breath. It was almost as though he were trying once more to kiss the crucifix and say, "I love you, Jesus," as he had done so often during life.

He had lived the teachings of the divine Master: "Take up your cross and follow Me." Now, at the very end of his life, in a final symbolic gesture this man of God literally took up his cross and followed Christ into eternity. He had already been anointed several times, and that morning was conscious enough to receive our divine Lord in Holy Viaticum for the last time. Now he was being welcomed home by this same divine giver of eternal life, Jesus Christ Himself.

May all of us, too, in whatever state of life we happen to be, have the courage and love to live and die for Christ—and in so doing, be His willing instruments in the greatest work of all—the salvation of souls.

God bless and keep you in His Sacred Heart now and forever.

17

Power of the Sacred Heart Badge

THE OFFICIAL Sacred Heart Badge of the Apostleship of Prayer has the image of our Lord on one side, showing us His Heart and pleading for our love just as He showed Himself to Saint Margaret Mary in the Visitation convent in France in 1674. On the other side of the badge is an image of the Sacred Heart, encircled with thorns, surmounted by a cross and flames of divine love. This side has the aspiration: "Cease, the Heart of Jesus is with me," and also the beautiful aspiration which expresses the zealous desire of every Apostle of Prayer: "Sacred Heart of Jesus, Thy Kingdom Come."

While members of the Apostleship of Prayer are not required to wear the Sacred Heart Badge, very many do wear it when receiving Holy Communion, especially on First Fridays, or when attending other public religious exercises. Many wear it during periods of illness or when they are seeking some special favor from the Sacred Heart of our divine Lord. There are many men and women who wear it secretly at all times and would not be without it. I would like to tell you now about a man who attributed the saving of his life [to] carrying the Sacred Heart Badge.

Several years ago I had the happiness of baptizing the fourth child of Ricky and Kris Nelson here in Los Angeles, California. I had married the young people some years before and had already baptized their three previous children. Ricky is the famous guitar player and singer, son of Ozzie and Harriet of TV fame, and Kris is the daughter of Tom and Elyse Harmon. Back in 1940, Tom Harmon was an All-American football star at University of Michigan, and at present is a renowned television sportscaster.

After the baptism, one of the older children of Ricky and Kris asked me to give him some kind of a remembrance of this happy occasion. He was the godfather of his little brother and wanted a keepsake. I took out of my pocket a Sacred Heart Badge and handed it to him and another to his brother and sister.

Tom Harmon, the grandfather, standing nearby, saw me do this and said to the little fellow: "Hang on to that Sacred Heart Badge. It will bring you through all kinds of difficulties and dangers as it did for me. I still have mine that I carried with me through the whole war, and I attribute to this Sacred Heart Badge the fact that I am alive today." Of course, I asked him to tell me his story, which he did.

"I was a pilot," he said, "and had been on many routine missions over enemy territory. I had to bail out twice, the second time being shot down by enemy Zeros at 500 feet. I pulled the ripcord, but the parachute didn't open. As I fell, my parachute caught in the trees, the jungle being so thick there. I attribute this saving of my life to the Sacred Heart Badge that I had in my pocket, for it was most strange to get caught up as I did. Then I started walking through the swampland of the jungle shouting "Hail Marys" at the top of my lungs. For six days I wallowed through the marshland, which was so thick and murky at times that I could hardly walk. Sometimes the oozy mud would be up to my knees, my waist, my neck, and even over my head. When it was over my head, I would go down as deep as I could until I touched solid ground. Then I would spring with as much power as I had at an angle in the direction I was going. I would catch a breath of air and then go down again repeating the same process over and over again, covering only a few feet at a time. I kept this up for those six days struggling through that horrible marshland. Finally, I came to an area where the more solid ground seemed to be on my left. I knew if I continued ahead in the direction I thought I should be going, I'd never make it. My strength was gone, and I was utterly exhausted. So I decided to go left and hope for the best. It was fortunate for me that I made such a decision, for if I had continued in the direction I had been going, I most certainly would have died. Again, I feel that the Sacred Heart Badge and my confidence in Christ's protection saved my life.

"Within a very short time the first sign of civilization appeared in the path ahead—a broken green bottle. Soon I reached a small village, the only friendly one within thirty-five miles. Thank God and the Sacred Heart that I am alive to tell you this experience."

We recall how our divine Lord promised in one of His apparitions to Saint Margaret Mary that He would bless every place where an image of His Sacred Heart was set up and honored. By having the Sacred Heart Badge in our possession, He is blessing each one of us in a special way.

God bless and keep you in His Sacred Heart now and forever.

18

My Most Loving Father

HOW CONSOLING IT IS TO REALIZE that God in Heaven, the all-wise and all-powerful Creator of everything in the universe, is also my own personal, loving Father. He loves me so much that, unlike all other creations in the world, He brought me into existence by a direct personal, individual act of His omnipotent will, and made me His image—a reflection of Himself.

A father's thought was in the mind of God and a father's feeling in the Heart of God when He came to the creation of me. He gave me a share, not only in His being, gave me not only life, but a share in His own life, so that I might not be just another creation but His child—and that forever.

What God willed in that act was that I might return filial love as a child to his Father. Endowing me with an intelligence to recognize Him as my loving Father, and a free will to accept Him as such, He has raised me up from the low level of my natural life into a participation in the splendor of His own divine and eternal life.

Incomprehensible as is this mystery of my Father's love for me, somehow in the infinite fullness of His life and goodness and joy, He was moved to share all these with me in order that I might give back the love of a child to his Father. Actually, this filial knowledge and love, by which I shall eternally glorify Him, will admit me into the complete possession and the very joy of God and the eternal living with Christ, His divine Son.

This is where I am going, not by the force of my own nature, but by the divine adoption of my Father in Heaven, who has taken this loving and marvelous way of drawing me into His life and eternal beatitude. No wonder Saint John could exclaim in wonderment, "Behold what manner of love the Father has bestowed upon us that we should be called the children of God; and such we are" (1 Jn 3:1). Saint Paul, too, over and over again speaks of our divine sonship, as he wrote to the Romans, "You have received a spirit of adoption as sons, by virtue of which we cry, 'Abba' (Father). For the Spirit Himself gives testimony to our spirit that we are the sons of God" (Rom 8:15–16).

God not only transmits to us His inheritance, for we are literally heirs of Heaven, His eternal kingdom, with Jesus Christ, His Son, but also as Saint Peter clearly states, "partakers of His divine nature" (2 Pt 1:4). By this, of course, we are not gods, but as His sons, we participate in His divine activity through the gift of sanctifying grace merited by the life and death of His Eternal Son, Jesus Christ.

Perhaps I might bring this point out by making a comparison. These days we are all quite accustomed to turning on our television set and channeling in the program we want to see at the moment. Now in order for the tube to light up, there has to be the electric current flowing through it, so we turn the switch and within a few moments it lights up. Then we tune in to the station we desire (in other words, we get on the right wavelength); for example, we channel into our home Heart of the Nation TV program or The Sacred Heart Hour, and there before us, we watch and hear a program dedicated to the Sacred Heart. The speaker appears there before us and tells us about "God, our loving Father," and we're thrilled to hear how much God loves us and has adopted us as His children.

Now, in somewhat of a like manner, we are God's television sets. In other words, when we have the current of sanctifying grace flowing through us, we light up with the Light of God dwelling in us. This is the switch that is turned on when we are baptized and is kept alive by staying out of serious sin. But in order to make sure that we are on God's wavelength, we channel our whole lives by the daily act of consecration through the Morning Offering. It is our heart tuning in to the Sacred Heart, for we, like our Brother, Jesus Christ, want everything we do or say or think—our prayers, works, joys, and sufferings—to be directed to the glory of God our Father in Heaven, the same as Jesus Christ Himself did when He was here on earth.

But when we turn on our television set, does the speaker actually come into our home? Is he there physically present in our parlor? No, of course not! But, by means of this scientific mechanical instrument, invented and perfected by men of learning, we participate in the activity, the operation of the speaker. He is able to multiply himself—bilocate, as it were—through these natural, material devices. Now, carrying out the comparison: what men have done on the natural level with material means, God, our heavenly Father, does on the supernatural level by means of sanctifying grace. His divine Son, Jesus Christ, takes up His life in us through this life of grace and bilocates Himself through our humanity. It is not that we are in any way equal to God, but He, our Loving Father, permits us to participate in His divine activity—His supernatural operations—through the indwelling of His divine Son. In other words, through this divine indwelling, He multiplies Himself over and over again, and today each one of us living in His friendship relives every phase of His life—His joyous, His sorrowful, and we shall also share in His glorious life—and that forever!

God bless and keep you in His Sacred Heart now and forever.

19

Our Own
Heavenly Father

DID YOU EVER STOP TO THINK what the opening words of the Lord's Prayer, "Our Father who art in Heaven," really mean? We are so accustomed to saying these words by memory that we scarcely ever take time to ponder their deeper meaning. "Our Father"—He is truly ours! We all know what the word, "Father," signifies in any language. "Father" means the head of the family, the one who watches over and protects his children, provides for them and makes sure that they are being taken care of in every way possible. A devoted father is one who sees a reflection of himself in his children, for they share his life and are everything to him. A loving father is glad to spend sleepless days and nights at the bedside of his little ones when they are ill—who would rather die himself than see his children suffer.

Why? Because these little ones are his own flesh and blood. As he looks upon his children, he sees himself, and every fiber of his father's heart goes out to them in love. Such a love is all-compelling, all-absorbing, self-sacrificing. How well this was brought home to me by the young father whom I saw in the hospital recovering from an accident. He was completely encased in a plaster cast from the top of his head down to his waist. All one could see of his face were the holes for his eyes, nose, and mouth.

Here was his story. He had been driving along with his small son at his side when the car hit some kind of an unexpected hazard in the road, causing it to swerve out of control and roll completely over. The boy was thrown out and lay unconscious in the ditch by the side of the road! In the father's anxiety for the life of his child, he paid no attention to himself, rushed over to the boy's side, picked him up, carried him back to the car and then drove some miles to the nearest town. There he brought the child into the local hospital where an immediate examination was made of the child's condition. When the doctor made his report to the father in these words, "Your son will live! He is not seriously injured!" the man's head fell into his hands! He had broken his neck! But in his agonizing concern over the boy, he completely forgot about his own sufferings. He felt nothing but the pain of his own child, but because of this very fact his own life was saved, for the muscles on both sides of his neck had so contracted from the nervous tension that they acted as a splint and held the bone in place. When he relaxed at the good news, he no longer had control over his head and had to bring his hands up to hold it in place. God was good to him, for the doctors took immediate action and saved his life.

Now if we can see such devotion and self-sacrificing love in a human father for his child, what must not be the driving love of our Father in Heaven for each one of us, His children here on earth! For this is the devotion of a God who loves man almost to folly; of a tender Father who is fairly captivated by the wiles of His little children; and yet of an omnipotent Father, Master of His household, who is so desperately in love with His own children that He made Himself man to bridge the distance between the infinite and the finite—so that man might be a partner in divinity. He is the God who loves man so much that He died of love. Truly, He is Our Father!

But the question is always being asked—how can this Eternal Father in Heaven love as insignificant a being as I am with such intensity? How can He be so interested in me personally as His own child, when there are so many millions of other people in the world? Yet, even if I were the only one in the whole world, God would not love me more than He loves me now! Why? Because our Heavenly Father, who loves infinitely and wisely, looks upon me as His own precious child, an individual imaging His glory. When God looks upon me He sees Himself in me, and with the entirety of His being turns to me in love. How He loves each of us!

All He wants in return is our love. His Sacred Heart pleads for our love. Remember, God our Father in Heaven can have anything and everything in this world at His slightest wish, but He cannot have our love unless we give it to Him.

God bless and keep you in His Sacred Heart now and forever.

20

The Apostleship of Prayer, a Way of Life

WHILE IN SAN FRANCISCO NOT LONG AGO, I crossed over the Golden Gate Bridge and the San Francisco-Oakland Bay Bridge. They are both tremendous structures built by man's scientific ingenuity and knowledge of engineering. Actually, it is breathtaking when you consider the tons and tons of weight these suspension bridges hold up.

As I glanced over the cables on each side, I thought to myself, "How strong these two cables must be in order to bear all this weight!" Yet I myself had watched the bridges being constructed some years ago, and I well remember how these cables had been woven together. First there was the catwalk, and the workers laboriously strung small strands one by one across the entire length of the bay from one tower to the other—and then to the deeply embedded anchors on either side.

Each strand in itself was not very strong, but after months of work stringing these small strands together they became a large, strong cable—now with strength to sustain the weight of the whole bridge and all the cars, trucks, and busses that were later to cross over it when completed.

In a somewhat parallel way, each one of us is like a single strand in the great cable that links us to God in Heaven—making a bridge between the finite and the infinite, between the creature and the Creator. Alone and by ourselves we may not be very much or very strong—in fact, we may be quite weak—but when there are many of us working and praying together, we become, as it were, like a strong cable forming a golden bridge by means of which men and women in this world are able to cross from this material existence of time to reach the joy and happiness of the Beatific Vision of God Himself for all eternity.

This is the idea of the Apostleship of Prayer! This is its very essence! In this "way of life," millions of people throughout the entire world of all races and colors are joined together like tiny strands with the daily Morning Offering. In this way they offer up their prayers, works, joys, and suffering of each day, thus transforming everything they do and think and say into a golden cable of spiritual, supernatural strength. In so doing they help one another to be better—to overcome evil—and ultimately save their souls and be with God forever in Heaven.

This is like the golden touch of King Midas. Everything he touched turned into gold. Through this daily offering, everything we touch turns into spiritual, supernatural gold, which cannot rust nor corrode. This is a type of currency that buys Heaven!

Some people have the idea that their prayer life is distinct and separate from the rest of their lives. They say to themselves, "I say my Our Fathers and Hail Marys. I said my Morning Prayers. Now I can go to work. Now I can clean the house. Now I can go to school. Now I can enjoy myself."

This is not true. Our prayer life goes hand in hand with our ordinary life. We don't say certain prayers and then put them high up on a shelf and say to ourselves, "I'm through praying for the day—now I'll go about my business." No! We are at prayer, or should be, not just when we are saying formal prayers or assisting at Holy Mass or making a visit to the Blessed Sacrament, but every second of the day should be a prayer, an offering to God, every minute, every hour—twenty-four hours out of the twenty-four! We are Christians, followers of Christ, Apostles of Prayer, every minute, waking or sleeping. We don't have to be at formal prayer to be prayerful. As long as we have the divine life of Christ dwelling within us through sanctifying grace, we are at prayer all the time and everything we do, no matter how prosaic or commonplace or ordinary it may be, becomes a prayer. Saint Paul tells us that whether we eat or drink or sleep or play, we should do all for the glory of God.

So it's not so important what we do, but why we do it—as our divine Lord Himself did during His life on earth. If we were to take a cross-section of His primitive life at Nazareth, we would see that everything heroic or extraordinary is ruled out. Jesus did the ordinary things of

His day but with purity of intention for the glory of His Eternal Father, the sanctification and salvation of all peoples everywhere. He was saving souls just as much at Bethlehem as a little baby in the crib as later on, when He was working miracles in the streets of Jerusalem or preaching from the mountainside. He was the Savior, an Apostle of Prayer, at Nazareth just as much as later on, when He was the Savior, and Apostle of Sacrifice, hanging on the cross of Calvary.

Through this gift of sanctifying grace that unites us to the divine, we too relive every phase of Christ's life in ours—His joyful, His suffering, and ultimately in the end, His glorious life. This is the Apostleship of Prayer—a way of life—in time and eternity.

God bless and keep you in His Sacred Heart now and forever.

21

Death—Resurrection Through the Spirit

WE ALL KNOW THAT ANY JOURNEY we make costs us something, and that if we expect to get somewhere, we have to pay the price for it. And the further the distance, the greater the price. But as long as we arrive at our destination, do we bemoan the fact that we had to put more gas in our tank, or that our tires wore down and had to be replaced, or that we had to relinquish our hard-earned money to pay for our train or airplane ticket? Of course not! We all realize that this is the price we have to pay in order to reach our journey's end.

So it is in regard to our journey here on earth towards our final destination. God placed us here on earth and breathed into our tiny little body a spiritual principle of life that destines each one of us for an immortal existence with Him in heaven. This is our whole purpose of life, and for this only we are destined by the nature God had given to us. We have been made by God, who endowed us with a spiritual nature like His own so that we could share with Him His own divine life and love for all eternity. Moreover, Jesus Christ, the eternal Son of God, became man and poured out His life's blood that we might be raised up to His divine life and enjoy supernatural happiness for all eternity.

With this awareness of our dignity as sons of God and the supernatural purpose of our life, is it not a logical conclusion to assert that we have to pay the price, or whatever is required, to reach this journey's end? I would certainly say so! And because it is beyond the reaches of this earth's atmosphere—beyond the almost limitless regions of the stars—up to the very infinite Being of God Himself, the easier it becomes. Now don't misunderstand me. I'm not saying that we still don't have to pay the price for reaching this heavenly goal, but we don't mind the cost at all—just as long as we get there.

Detachment from the things of earth is the beginning and perhaps the hardest struggle of all, but living a supernatural life by Faith makes it far easier to be willing to pay the price, cost what it may. It is something like our gigantic rockets that the government spends billions of dollars in constructing for the purpose of putting men on the moon, and later on Venus and Mars—and on and on. The government doesn't mind spending these billions in the hope that this project will be a success and will accomplish the purpose for which these mighty rockets and intricate scientific machines and instruments have been built.

Getting the rocket ship off the earth and out of this world's atmosphere is the most difficult part of the operation. It takes tremendous power and energy to lift these tons of machinery off their pad, and the initial thrust generates enough power to light up a dozen cities. But once the capsule is launched into the airless regions of outer space, no power at all is required to keep it going in its orbit around the earth.

I would say that it is much the same with man. If we are to rise with Christ and share with Him His eternity of happiness, then we have to be willing to leave behind the things of time, which weigh us down to earth, and generate enough power by the grace of God to let Him lift us up out to the weather-less, supernatural regions where we can view all things with the thoughts of God, and see everything in its rightful perspective.

Certainly the astronauts soaring some four to five hundred miles up above the earth can more clearly appreciate the smallness of man in himself without God and the final purpose for which He created him. The higher up we go in our relationship to God through prayer and union with Him, by keeping our souls in His grace and love, the clearer also becomes our supernatural insight into all that God has prepared for those that love Him. In other words, the higher up we go in our efforts to keep close to God in time, even though this demands a constant death to self, the vaster becomes our vision of the emptiness of material things and the more intimate becomes our union with God through His Holy Spirit dwelling within our souls.

Then it is that our whole life is ruled by love, which makes us want to do only those things which please God. This becomes like an inward drive where we lose all taste for sin and we are bent upon doing only that which pleases our Father in Heaven. The divine indwelling of the Holy Spirit gives this initial thrust to our life, lifting us up to the life of God, and continues to strengthen us in our daily efforts to relive the glorious life of our Risen Savior in us and through us, every moment of our life, until at long last He calls us home to be happy with Him forever in Heaven.

God bless and keep you in His Sacred Heart now and forever.

22

Hope For Nations

ONE CAN TRULY SAY that the love of the Sacred Heart for all mankind throughout the world today is just as strong and vibrant as it was when our divine Lord walked this earth of ours. Just as at that time He gathered together the people on the mountainside, or by the Lake of Gennesaret, and held them spellbound with His words, "I have come that you may have life and have it more abundantly" (Jn 10:10); "I am the way, the truth and the life" (Jn 14:6), so to all the peoples of the world today, He proclaims once again that He is the only hope for all nations everywhere.

While mighty ambassadors from various nations of the world gather in New York at the United Nations headquarters in an effort to bring about a lasting peace in the world, He, the Prince of Peace, has long since announced His program for a deep-down peace in the hearts of men. The angels chanted it at His birth: "Glory to God in the highest and peace on earth to men of good will" (Lk 2:14).

Here is the secret of peace—here is the hope of nations—found in the Heart of God who was urged to become a tiny Babe in the manger of Bethlehem; to allow Himself to be born in poverty, humiliation, and suffering; to live a life of obscurity, silence, work, and obedience during thirty years of His hidden life; to go out into a waiting world and endure the calumnies, mockeries, and insults of three years of public life; and then to tread the wine press of bitter suffering in His Passion, Crucifixion and death on the cross—all for one reason—because He loved man—all men of all nations—and each man in particular with such a gnawing zeal that it all but consumed Him.

In our anxious world of today, His Heart is fairly bursting within His breast as He calls out to each weary soul, "Come unto Me all you who are weary and find life burdensome and I will sustain you, for My yoke is sweet and My burden light" (Mt 11:28). In my meditation I can almost hear Him say,

> I have truth in every word I say, and I will show you the way to life everlasting. Have confidence; I have overcome the world. My attitude of living will bring you peace. Blessed are the poor in spirit, the meek, and they that mourn; blessed are they that hunger and thirst after justice, the merciful, the pure of heart and the peacemakers; blessed are they that suffer persecution for justice's sake. Blessed are you when they shall revile you and persecute you and speak all that is evil against you, untruly, for my sake. Be glad and rejoice, for your reward is very great in heaven.

By these words does He promise a good time here on earth? No! But He does promise a good eternity. Does He promise temporal or material goods or joys? No! Does He say life here on earth is a path of roses? No! But He does say, "Take up your cross and follow Me." And He promises unending happiness in Heaven for those who do so. "Well done, my good and faithful servant," He says in anticipation to each one, "come, share your Master's joy" (Mt 25:21).

Then He commanded His Ambassadors to go to every corner of the world and teach these lessons to all who would listen. "All power in heaven and on earth has been given to me. Go, therefore, and make disciples of all nations, baptizing them in the name of the Father, and of the Son, and of the Holy Spirit, teaching them to observe all that I have commanded you. And behold, I am with you always, until the end of the age" (Mt 28:16–20).

Truly, here is a program that will bring peace to the world; here is a way of life for all nations to live together in mutual trust and harmony—not to look down to the material passing world so fleeting and insecure, but to look up to Christ, the Prince of Peace, and to the spiritual eternal kingdom He offers to those who live for Him and follow His way of life—His Beatitudes!

No wonder that Pope Leo XIII, in the year 1899, ordered the consecration of the entire world to the Sacred Heart, proclaiming His divine Heart the symbol and sensible image of the infinite love of

Jesus Christ, the only source of lasting peace—the hope for nations.

Today, ambassadors gathering together on opposite sides of a table at the United Nations Headquarters are striving to devise ways and means of effecting a lasting peace, but, sadly enough, they leave out of their calculations the very source of peace—God Himself. How can man have peace without its source?

But thank God, there are other people from all nations of the world who gather together on opposite sides of another table. This table is the altar of the Lord, and on the other side is the dwelling place of the Prince of Peace Himself, our Lord and Savior, Jesus Christ. And there His Sacred Heart is throbbing with love for everyone today, just as strongly as when He lived here on earth.

No words can better express this thought than those of Pope Leo XIII in His memorable encyclical, Annum Sacrum,

when the Church, in the days immediately following her institution was oppressed beneath the yoke of the Caesar, a young emperor saw in the heavens a cross, which became at once the happy omen and cause of the glorious victory that soon followed. And now, today, behold! another blessed and heavenly token is offered to be our sign: the Most Sacred Heart of Jesus, with a cross rising from it and shining forth with dazzling splendor amidst flames of love. In that Sacred Heart all our hopes should be placed, and from it the salvation of men is to be sought with confidence!

God bless and keep you in His Sacred Heart now and forever.

23

Jesus Christ,
the Heavenly Astronaut

WHAT A THRILLING SIGHT it was to watch our astronauts—for the first time in the history of the world—place their feet upon the surface of the moon! Truly, it was a breathtaking spectacle to see these men walk about on its eerie terrain and then go about their duties, wasn't it? The moon would no longer be the same, because it had been touched by man. Then we watched them as they gathered up the dust from the moon's surface and carried it back to their return space ship. We had never before seen anything like it as they planted the American flag and saluted it in allegiance to their country. From that moment on the moon would never be the same, because it had been touched by man. It was now man's moon—he had conquered it!

Almost two thousand years ago there was another Astronaut, a heavenly one, who for the first time in the history of man touched the surface of this earth, and from that moment on, it was never to be the same because it had been touched by a Man who was different from every other man who ever lived. This one was greater than man because He was the eternal Son of God, Jesus Christ, one with the Father from all eternity who became man in time. He touched the surface of this earth, and from that time on it was never the same again because it had been sanctified by the touch of the God who created it. He had conquered it!

This heavenly Astronaut also had a task to accomplish. Being obedient to His Father in Heaven, He went about His mission of redeeming man. He, too, gathered up the dust from the surface of the earth, and taking it to His Heart, sanctified it by His touch and blessed it. His

Heart was pierced as He hung on the cross of Calvary, and His Precious Blood flowed down upon the dust which He had sanctified—and it became holy dust touched by the Blood of Christ.

For this dust is but you and I! Remember, on Ash Wednesday at the beginning of Lent, the priest takes the ashes and makes the Sign of the Cross over our forehead with them and says, "Remember, man, thou art dust, and unto dust thou shalt return." Yes, we are the dust that Jesus Christ has sanctified by His touch. We have been made holy because He has given us His own divine life by shedding His Blood and dying for us.

Just as the astronauts from earth brought back to this world the dust from the moon, and it became a treasure of great value to men of science, so this heavenly Astronaut is bringing back each one of us to the infinite realms of God Himself, where we shall continue to be His treasure throughout the eons of eternity. Through His infinite merits by His becoming man and dying on the cross for each one of us, He has lifted us up to a participation in His own divine life.

Men and women of all generations, each one of us reading these words and I myself, are we not all but dust vivified by the personal love of God in creating our immortal soul? Are we not now the adopted children of our heavenly Father, destined for an eternal oneness with Him in the Beatific Vision—all because Jesus Christ, the Son of God, was willing to die that we might live?

And even beyond this, can I not in all truth say that my tongue becomes an altar of the Lord, my heart His sanctuary lamp, my whole body His living tabernacle—His living chalice—since I in a very special way have been touched by His Body and Blood, Soul and Divinity, through the gateway of the Holy Eucharist? Truly, how sacred my whole being is now that I have been sanctified by the touch of divinity! I am no longer the same because the earth of my mortal body has been nourished by the very God who brought it into existence.

There is no greater union than that between myself and the food I eat, and as a result, my blood in a mysterious, supernatural way mingles with His Blood; my heart palpitates with every beat of His; my soul through this heavenly banquet is able to leap out of itself like a rocket up beyond the outer stratosphere of this earth—beyond the farthest star in the heavens—to the infinite, uncreated kingdom of

God Himself, where deified as a son of God by grace, I shall share with Him His peace and joy and love with all the saints and angels in Heaven forever.

God bless and keep you in His Sacred Heart now and forever.

24

Love Finds Christ

SINCE THE DAWN OF MAN'S HISTORY, love has been the dominating force in the lives of all peoples everywhere. It has moved young and old alike to endure every kind of hardship, suffering, torture, even death itself for the one loved. Truly has it been said that of all human experiences, there is none stronger nor more powerful to move hearts and minds than that of love.

But what really is this love of which we speak that has such power over the lives of men? When we analyze it deeply, we cannot help but draw the conclusion that this all-powerful force firing up the hearts of all is something which only man, God's image—sharing His qualities of spirit—can possess. For this love is an intellectual appreciation of the other person's worth—that the beloved is altogether lovable in himself and worthy of a willing return of love. It does not concern itself so much with mere externals, such as a beautiful body or a handsome face; much less is it a mere physical attraction or infatuation.

This love goes deep down into the very spirit of a person and rests primarily in the will—not the emotions. It is perceiving spiritual qualities in the one loved which make him lovable—that he possesses in himself such goodness, generosity, purity, self-sacrifice, and so much more—that one cannot help but be overpowered by this captivating person. There rises within his soul an ardent desire to make a return of love, cost what it may.

With these thoughts in mind of what spiritual love really means, now we can readily understand how it is that men and women through all ages have fallen in love with Jesus Christ. In Him they find the very epitome of all perfection and have become intellectually aware of His captivating Personality. He becomes everything to them, the very center of their lives here on earth, and gives meaning to all they do.

God's saints, the greatest hero-worshipers of all time, have seen in this Man, who was really greater than man because He is the eternal Son of God, qualities that have impelled them to give their all for Him—to pour out their life's blood like water, to endure the rack and the rope, to be torn apart by wild beasts, to be crucified and set on fire with hot pitch rather than deny Him. Their love, today as always, has become so boundless that there could never be any sacrifice too great that they would not be willing to make to prove their love for Him. Studying His life here on earth, they have gotten to know Him intimately, and knowing Him have fallen desperately in love with Him. And once such a love has caught hold, there is nothing—no, nothing—even life itself—that they would ever hold back from giving Him.

They see in Him absolute sinlessness, wisdom proverbial in His own day, limitless charity, kindness beyond description, mercy and compassion, understanding of His fellowman's weakness and a gracious pity projecting itself into each one's needs, and a constant outpouring of love in selfless sacrifice that led all the way from Bethlehem to Calvary. He was always giving love and never demanding it in return. Having all these attractive human qualities of perfection would be enough to cause anyone's heart to leap up in loyalty and service of such a wonderful man—but He has infinitely more because He is also divine, and being divine He has power omnipotent and can promise an award of everlasting joy with Him in His kingdom.

Christ's hero-worshipers are convinced that in following and loving this divine Master and putting His ideals of human living into their own, they will find Christ and have the happiness of sharing with Him His unending love for all eternity. Saint Teresa of Avila in her autobiography tells us that our Risen Savior once appeared to her in vision, and that if there were no other joy in Heaven than the contemplation of the humanity of Christ, this alone would constitute a delight beyond human words to describe.

No wonder Father Willie Doyle, the famous Irish chaplain who was killed in action in Flanders in 1917 during the First World War, exclaimed in his most ardent prayer:

Jesus is the most loving of lovable friends. There never can be one to equal Him, because there is only one Jesus in the whole wide world and the vast expanse of Heaven, and that sweet loving Friend, that true Lover of the holiest and purest love is My Jesus, mine alone and all mine. Every fiber of His divine nature is thrilling with love for me, every beat of His gentle Heart is a throb of intense affection for me, His sacred arms are around me, He draws me to His breast, He bends down with infinite tenderness over me, His child, for He knows I am all His, and He is all mine. In His eyes the vast world, the myriads of other souls have all vanished, He has forgotten them all—for that brief moment they do not exist—for even the infinite love of God Himself is not enough to pour out on the soul who is clinging so lovingly to Him.

God bless and keep you in His Sacred Heart now and forever.

25

Preparation for the Work of the Gospel

IF ONE IS TO BE A TRUE and effective apostle of Jesus Christ and carry out His final command to go into the whole world and teach all nations, then he must be completely filled up in his own personal life with Christ's thinking, teaching, and way of doing things. He will be a useful instrument only insofar as he puts on Christ and permits Him to "take over" and continue reliving Christ's life in his. In other words, by becoming Christlike in all that he does and by choosing the same means to this end that Christ chose in His, then and only then will he be able to bring others to the true knowledge and love of the truths that are contained in the Word of God—the Gospel message that there is faith and hope and love, and that God has created us, not just to live for a moment of time, but to be eternally happy with Him in Heaven.

Preparation for such a noble apostolic career means that one must learn how the divine Apostle prepared Himself for the work His Father had given Him to do. How did He go about preparing Himself for the task of influencing people everywhere in all the ages to come? Did He come with great armies and material weapons to conquer and bend the wills of others to His own? No! Christ came into this world with a challenge, but not to conquer people by the force of arms or compel them to obey His holy will. He came with the utter simplicity of a helpless baby to win over the hearts of all who would contemplate the God of all creation lying on the straw of a manger, cuddled in the arms of His Mother. With one gesture, He overthrew the false standard of the world which holds that to conquer others one has to be mighty and powerful and seemingly very important in the eyes of men.

107

As He grew up from babyhood through childhood to His manhood, what manner of life did He choose to prepare Himself for the great work His Father had given Him to do—to form the minds and wills of others so that they would not be captivated by the passing trivialities of earthly time, but would look up and embrace the truths of eternal value?

Again, we see Christ during the thirty years at Nazareth living very simply and humbly with His own family, as any other young man of his time would do. It was a life of obedience, humility, work, and submission.

"Dear Lord," we ask, "is this Your way of preparing Yourself for the most important work of all—the salvation of souls? Aren't You wasting precious years of time? After all, Lord, You haven't many more years left, You know. It seems to me that You could be accomplishing a great deal more for souls by going out right away and preaching the Gospel message. Think of all the people who are dying during these years and need Your help."

In my prayer I imagine Christ would answer me, "Remember, I'm not out for a spectacular program. My Father in Heaven doesn't measure the number of people one contacts or the number of miles one travels. If He wants things done in a hurry, He can effect them in an instant. But to be a fitting instrument as My apostle, you must model your life on Mine. It's not important what you do, but why you do it that counts in God's eyes. It's purity of intention and motivation that really counts in the light of eternity."

No matter how commonplace or ordinary our business, job, or home life may be, like Christ at Nazareth with Saint Joseph and His Mother, Mary, we can be very happy in the realization that as far as the salvation of souls is concerned, everything is of value in God's plan. We, like Christ, can be preparing ourselves as His missionaries behind an office desk or mopping a floor, cooking a dinner or driving a car, on a bed of pain or playing a game, knowing now that it's not what we do, but why we do it that counts in God's eyes.

I like to imagine Jesus Christ saying His daily Morning Offering prayer before every action of the day during all the years of his life: from the manger to the cross; in the quiet solitude of Nazareth or in the heated arguments with the learned men of the Old Law.

It is too bad that some people miss their golden opportunity of greatness and doing magnificent work for God by not finding it in the prosaic, day-by-day events of life with their own family, husbands, wives, children, their work, and the people they daily rub shoulders with. This is what Christ did.

It is not to find possible greatness elsewhere outside of ourselves, but within our own small humble state of life, whatever that might be. It is the daily conviction that happiness is not in making progress for human welfare, but for the never-ending happiness with God our Father in Heaven for all eternity.

God bless and keep you in His Sacred Heart now and forever.

26

The Best of Friends

THERE IS A WELL-KNOWN EXPRESSION which states, "Tell me who your friends are, and I'll tell you what you are." How true this saying is, for we all know that the kind of man we choose for a friend, and the kind of woman too, will be a sure guide of some sort as to the kind of man or woman we are ourselves. Therefore, to develop a successful personality in the eyes of God, it is a mark of wisdom to cultivate good supernatural friends. Of course there is One over and above all friends. He is the best possible Friend we can ever have, both in time and for eternity. This Friend is the God-man, Jesus Christ. He bridged the infinite distance between God and man by becoming man Himself in order that through His humanity, we might be able to develop a friendship with God.

Our divine Lord desires all men to love Him ardently and be close to His Sacred Heart. "I have come," He said, "to set the earth on fire, and how I wish it were already blazing" (Lk 12:49). To have this fire of love for Him, our best Friend, burning in our hearts, we must first get to know Him well and intimately. And just as we derive no end of joy from the mere thought of someone we love, so in our effort to know Him better, our hearts are filled to overflowing in happy contemplation of this wonderful friend of ours.

What kind of a man was Jesus Christ? We are all hero-worshipers of one kind or another. The human heart loves a conqueror, because the human heart was made to win. But alas for this human heart of ours made to win, is constantly losing—made to thrill in the thought of victory, it suffers almost universal defeat. Where now are the conquerors of the past? Look back through the long corridor of the centuries. They will tell you the true story of human greatness. Cemeteries' dust waves requiem over the heroes of the past, and only the epitaph, "Here he lies" marks the crumbling spot where conquered conquerors repose. And yet in their day, each was a great hero to those who followed him.

Where then shall we find a hero who will not and cannot be conquered? I'll tell you where the saints of God found Him, and where each one of us can find our Hero and Friend who will never let us down. That Hero is Jesus Christ, the most wonderful Man who ever lived. He was really more than man, because He was the Son of God! We call Him Jesus of Nazareth—the God-man. We study Him and find that here at last is our ideal of perfect manhood—without a blemish!

We admire Him for His intelligence. Even in His own day, the people were in awe at His doctrine and whispered to one another, "No man ever spoke as this man." At the age of twelve He answered the questions of the doctors and learned men of the Law and left them utterly bewildered! The Pharisees planned to catch Him in His speech and trap Him when they cunningly asked Him such questions as, "Is it lawful to render tribute to Caesar?" But He cut their dilemmas in half by answering, "Render unto Caesar the things that are Caesar's, and unto God the things that are God's" (Mt 22:21). He spoke with such winning wisdom that five thousand men followed Him out into a desert, and for three days forgot to eat, so engrossed did they become in the words of wisdom that flowed from the lips of this great teacher.

The doctrine He established and His moral code of conduct still stand out against the horizon of the centuries like a rock-ribbed Gibraltar, against whose immovable base all opposing doctrines dash themselves to vaporous nothingness. With this friend of ours, we always know where we stand and what He expects of us.

We admire Him further for the tenderness of His love which was all-embracing, disinterested, and self-sacrificing. He loved all men, even His enemies. He loved unto death, even to the death of the cross. As we learn to know Him better, how can we help but be carried away in our desire to develop this friendship? This is what happened to the saints as a spark of love burst into an all-consuming flame in their eagerness to put our divine Lord and His ideals into their lives. "Christ was tender in His love—self-sacrificing—all-embracing—willing to pour out His life's blood for His fellow man. Then, that is for me!

What was good enough for Christ is good enough for me. I'll wash the beggars' rags! I'll comfort the sick and suffering! I'll bathe the lepers' sores! I'll dig graves and bury the dead! Why, I will go to the ends of the world to be like Christ! I must become Christlike—think like Christ, act like Christ, breathe Christ and be another Christ! I must relive Christ's life in mine!" Such a friendship fired the heart of Saint Paul with such burning love that he cried out, "I live—no, not I, but Christ lives in me" (Gal 2:20). "Gladly, therefore, will I glory in my infirmities that the strength of Christ may dwell in me" (2 Cor 12:9).

Truly, here is the sure way of developing a successful personality, both here in time and for eternity—to be one in heart and mind and will with the best of friends, our divine Savior, Jesus Christ! For this friend is the way, the truth, and the life who will lead us through the darkness to the light; from the dross of this world to the beauty and power and majesty of Heaven everlasting.

God bless and keep you in His Sacred Heart now and forever.

27

A Model in Christ

HOW FORTUNATE WE ARE to live in the world of today with all of its scientific achievements and unbelievable conquests of outer space! Why, within our own lifetime we have seen so many breathtaking, spell-binding spectaculars that utterly baffle our imagination to picture.

Yet all this is as nothing compared to what took place almost two thousand years ago when Jesus Christ, the Son of God, broke through the limitless barrier between the un-created and the created, between the infinite and the finite, between the supernatural and the natural, between God and man—and linked humanity to divinity by becoming man Himself. From that heavenly earthshaking event, human nature would never be the same, for now it is deified—lifted up to the supernatural plane of God Himself and a participant in God's own divine nature.

Since God became man and lived the same human life as we do from birth to death, our own existence and living takes on new meaning. Now we have the ideal of human nature in Christ, and the whole effort and work on our part is to model our lives on His and become Christlike. "I am the way and the truth and the life," He tells us. "No one comes to the Father save through Me" (Jn 14:6). "I am the light of the world. Whoever follows Me will not walk in darkness but will have the light of life" (Jn 8:12). We study Christ in His human nature so that we can know how to live a godly life through Him and with Him and in Him. Before the coming of Christ, God was conceived as being rather distant—a sort of faraway God, a rather unapproachable, perhaps a little fearsome, and awe-inspiring deity—one who loved man, but still a God of fear.

Then when Christ came into this world, man was able to see God in action, cloaked in the same human nature but still remaining God. He came to earth from Heaven so that man might be able to have a faint glimpse of what that Heaven must be—the complete oneness with all he yearns for, to be found only in God Himself. By becoming man, Christ brought this knowledge within reach of the mind of man. He came out of the eons of forever so that we might be able to make a loving and joyous contact with the infinite, which otherwise would have been impossible. In short, Jesus Christ, the God who became man, did so in order that He might raise us up to divinity, which we could never have done alone.

Now with Christ in our midst we have security and comforting peace in knowing that by following His example, we are definitely carrying out God's holy will and eventually will have the consummation of union with Him forever. Since there is no other way except through Him, our perfect way of human living here on earth is to become more and more Christlike—Christ-loving and Christ-living. Our constant refrain in prayer must be that we get to know Christ, and knowing Him, to love Him, and loving Him, to imitate and follow His example, for He has come to teach us how to live and above all, how to love.

In such a short talk as this, it would be utterly impossible to describe all the heart-warming, lovable qualities in Christ which we should strive daily to put into our own lives, so perhaps I'll just emphasize a few that have helped me along the way. First of all, Christ was absolutely sinless. He came into this world to carry out His Father's will, even though it cost Him His life. So if I am to keep this ideal of being Christlike before my mind, I too must be as sinless as possible and strive daily to carry out God's will in all I do.

Then there is that inspiring virtue of courage that we see exemplified in Christ. He was a man of character at all times, dominating His life by principles. When He knew something was right in the eyes of His Father, He would stand firm as a rock and would not budge, no matter what the price He personally had to pay for doing what He knew had to be done. So often, Christ is pictured as a sort of weakling, a milk-soppy character, because He taught kindness and love and mercy. Those who portray him this way confuse weakness with meekness. Christ was meek, but He was not weak.

But one quality in Christ above all that has knocked down all the barriers is His deep understanding of human nature and its weaknesses. He could not stand evil, but He loved the sinner. No matter who came to Him, if he were the vilest perpetrator of evil in the whole world, Christ would always welcome Him back to His Heart and forgive him all if he were truly sorry for having offended God. He was tender in His consideration of everyone, and all felt the warmth of His loving personality.

So if I am to be another Christ in the world of today, if I am truly to relive His life in mine, then I too must do God's holy will, as He did, before all else.

God bless and keep you in His Sacred Heart now and forever.

28

Special Love of Jesus for Little Children

AS WE STUDY the life of our divine Master, we find that He had a special place in His Heart for little children. It was His delight to be in their midst—to romp and play with them and have them clamor around His knee as He told them stories in simple language of the love of God. He laid His hands upon them and on occasion, embraced and blessed them. I like to imagine His curing the paralyzed, crippled bodies of His little ones, then picking them up on His shoulders and running up and down along the shore of Lake Gennesaret as He explains to them the beauty and majesty of God in every drop of water and grain of sand—or touching the eyes of little blind children and watching their expression of joy as, wide-eyed, they look into His smiling face. How our divine Savior loved little children! When His apostles tried to shoo them away, feeling they were annoying Him, He gently reprimanded them for their unwarranted concern. "Suffer the little children to come unto Me, and forbid them not, for of such is the kingdom of God" (Lk 18:16). How highly He valued their purity of soul and angelic innocence He proved when, holding a child close to His Heart, He said to His disciples: "Amen, I say to you, unless you become converted and become as little children, you shall not enter the kingdom of Heaven. Whosoever therefore shall humble himself as this little child, he is the greater in the kingdom of Heaven. And he that shall receive one such child as this, receives Me."

Never once did He ever scold a child, nor hesitate to take time out to be with them. And when they would come to Him with their little toys and playthings, He would be as interested in those as though the most important event of history was taking place.

Is it any wonder then, that when our divine Lord instituted the sacrament of the Holy Eucharist, He was eager to have little children through all the ages of Christianity welcome Him often in Holy Communion! He yearns to be close to them today, just as much as He did centuries ago when He was here on earth in His humanity. No one knows better than He that those little ones of His would always be a source of consolation to His bleeding Heart when they would become one with Him, through the Living Bread of His own Body and Blood in Holy Communion.

There lived a little boy some years ago who seemed to be very intimately aware of this close union between our Savior and himself, and even though he was only five years old, he had a burning desire to receive Him in Holy Communion. Frankie—that was his name— was the oldest of four children and with his golden locks looked just like a picture of the Christ Child. The little boy had a deep insight into the love of the Sacred Heart and had expressed his desire to be a priest from the age of two. His Mother made him vestments with a golden chasuble like a priest wears at Mass, and of course he had a play altar. It was heartwarming to watch the little fellow as he pretended he was saying Mass. He would turn around with his arms wide and say: Dominus vobiscum (for Mass was said in Latin at that time), which means, "The Lord be with you," like a priest at the altar. One day while I was visiting the family, he delivered a sermon on the love of our divine Savior that fairly took my breath away. In his childlike expression, he compared God to Santa Claus. "You know," he said, "at Christmas time, Santa comes down the chimney and brings us all kinds of toys and things to make us happy, but Santa wouldn't have any toys at all to give away unless God first made the trees from which he could put the toys together." It was beautiful!

God must have loved Frankie very much, for He wanted him all for Himself—to be right in His Sacred Heart—as His little tabernacle. The child was suddenly stricken with a very serious disease and within a few days was lying next to death's door in the hospital. They had him in an oxygen tent, and for a while, he was able to pretend he was a soldier fighting for his King. He clenched a small crucifix in his tiny fist until he was too weak to hold it any longer—then a nurse pinned it to his pillow and he was satisfied. When she asked him what he wanted to be when he grew up, he answered, "I want to be a priest!" "Why?" the nurse asked. "Because I want to hold the Baby Jesus up as a priest does at Mass—because I love the Baby Jesus."

Frankie's Baby Jesus must have loved him very much, because He came all the way down from Heaven—the child made his First Holy Communion on his deathbed—and then the Lord of Heaven and earth held His little Frankie by the hand and took him up to Heaven. Frankie died—yes—but he died in the embrace of the one whom he loved above all else—our divine Jesus, who has time and time again manifested His special love for little children. This little boy desired to receive Holy Communion so ardently that our Loving Savior could not resist his prayer. A little angel left this materialistic world to fly into the very Heart of Jesus to be with Him for all eternity.

All of us can derive a lesson from this, for if we become as little children—small in our own eyes, but big in the eyes of God—we too will radiate His love and have a special place in His Sacred Heart—now and always.

God bless and keep you in His Sacred Heart now and forever.

29

My Heavenly Brother

JESUS CHRIST IS MY BROTHER! I know He is my Brother because we both have the same Father in Heaven. He is the only begotten Son of the Father, and I, His son by adoption. We both have the same divine life flowing through our souls: He by right of His divine nature; I, because my Brother merited it for me by becoming man and living here on earth and then dying for me on the cross. He took my place so that I might be raised up to the same divine life that He possesses for all eternity. He is my Brother who loves me so much that He exchanged His divinity for my humanity—so that we both might call upon His Eternal Father as OUR Father.

What a Brother I have in Jesus Christ! There is a familiar saying that a brother helped by a brother is like a strong city. I cannot help but think of how much my brother has helped me and all that He has done for me. He not only lived and worked for me, but He died for me. And greater love than this no man has: that he be willing to die for his friend—his brother.

Perhaps an illustration might help to bring this point out. During the war, when the soldiers who had been wounded in battle were sent back to various hospitals and rest homes to convalesce, the story is told of how one of these young men lay unconscious in critical condition next to death's door. His little brother sat at his side holding his hand and praying as though to give strength to the older boy. The doctor standing whispered, "The only thing that can save this man's life is an immediate transfusion of living blood."

The boy's face brightened as he cried out eagerly, "Doctor, I'll give my blood for my brother."

"All right, son," was the doctor's answer, "come into the next room and we'll see if your blood is of the same type as your brother's."

They hurriedly stepped out and took the quick test, found that the two bloods perfectly matched, and then went ahead with the operation. As it was going on and as the little boy's blood coursed into the veins of his brother, one could see new life blossoming in the face of the older man. When it was all over, the little fellow kept lying there. "You can get up now, son," the doctor said, "the operation is all over."

"What do you mean, doctor—isn't my blood good enough?"

"Why, yes, but we've taken all that's necessary. Your blood has saved the life of your brother." Tears trickled down the cheeks of the boy as he haltingly asked, "You mean I'm not going to die?"

The doctor drew back in amazement, "Do you mean to tell me that when you lay down there next to your brother you thought you were going to die?"

"Yes, doctor," came the quick reply, "I thought I was going to give all my blood for my brother."

Our Brother, Jesus Christ, was not only willing to give His life's Blood for His brothers and sisters—all of us—but He actually poured out every drop of it to prove how great was His love for each member of His family—each one of us.

This was the only law that He had—the law of love. He wanted us to love God above all else; to love our neighbor, no matter how poor and lowly; and to love even our enemies. He held high the value of being little—to be meek and kind and forgiving in a world that was cruel and hard-hearted. He taught how to find happiness in the lasting things of the spirit and not to center one's hopes on the passing trivialities of this life that go up in smoke and last only for an hour. He drove home time and again the lesson that man was created, not for an earthly paradise that crumbles into the dust, but for membership in His own family in the kingdom of His Eternal Father forever. He condemned anything that would take man's eyes away from this goal. Pride and greed and envy and hypocrisy and impurity and all other evils—these must go! And He proved the value of this way of life not just by preaching it, but by living it, and in the end by dying for it.

Sometimes my Brother is caricatured as a weakling. Some say His doctrine is for the dreamer or the anemic or the aesthetic, but not for men of vitality and strength. This is not true! These people mistake meekness for weakness. Christ was anything but weak, and His doctrine demands courage. He was no weakling! He was a man of character. He came into this world with a challenge, and when it was a question of carrying out His Father's will, He stood firm as a rock and would not budge, no matter if it cost His life. He preached fearlessly by word and example, prayed through long hours of the night, cured the sick and brought the dead back to life, walked on the waters and calmed the seas, fed the crowd miraculously in the desert and travelled from one end of Palestine to the other. He endured weariness, hunger, thirst and could still love and forgive when His back was purpled with welts from the scourging, His head crowned with thorns, and His Body nailed to a cross!

My Brother a weakling? No! He was a man with the strength of God Himself and with a Heart pierced by a lance so that He might pour out His Precious Blood for me—His brother—He gave his Blood that I might live.

God bless and keep you in His Sacred Heart now and forever.

30

My Brother in Heaven

DID YOUR HEART ever burst with happiness? Mine did the other evening while listening to some very beautiful music. While the heavenly notes filled the room, my imagination carried me away to the joys of being with our Savior in Heaven. I thought of Him just as a Brother—my own brother!

It was like this. He met me with the most captivating smile and then took my arm in His as we two, side by side, joyously ran through the corridors of Heaven. I don't think I've ever felt so happy in my life to know my Brother was right there at my side. It seemed as though He took pride in showing me around and introducing me to this one and that one, each a member of His family. Saint Peter, to my right, took my hand and welcomed me, and Saint Paul, too, greeted me with a gesture of "Well done, apostle, I liked the way you put over the same message that I used with the early Corinthians—you know, comparing the Church to the physical body made up of many members with one head, all having the welfare of the whole body." It made me feel pretty good to get this pat on the back from the greatest apostle of them all, for I knew how much our Brother, Jesus Christ, loved him for all he had accomplished for Him.

Oh, there were any number of thrills as He took me around, having me next meet Saint Francis Xavier. It gave me a chance to ask him how in the world he had been able to baptize so many thousands of pagans in India, Japan, and other places of the Far East in such a short time. Of course his answer was a very knowing wink and a quiet chuckle as his eye caught our Brother's standing there beside us. It was as though they had a secret between them, and yet I knew exactly what they meant. Saint Paul would probably have said, "Not I—it's Christ living in me" (Gal 2:20) or "I can do all things in Him who strengthens me" (Phil 4:13).

There were many others we met in our happy childlike journey arm in arm, my Brother and I, like Saint Gertrude, Saint Mechtilde, Saint John Eudes, Saint Margaret Mary, all of whom seemed to radiate a certain warmth of peace and love—as though even in Heaven in my Brother's home, they still felt the fiery pulsations of His Sacred Heart—and to tell me more about His love. But something distracted me for the moment. I perceived the most delicious, delicate, heavenly incense fragrance floating over toward me from somewhere. I turned around, and there right at my back was Saint Aloysius Gonzaga. Was I glad to meet him! I told him how I had carried his relic around my neck for years and how he had constantly helped me in retreats, sermons, problems and what not—and how grateful I was to him for all he did for me. He was triumphantly happy to welcome me into our Brother's house—really made me feel right at home.

Then who should come skipping up to greet us, but the Little Flower, Saint Thérèse herself! What a beautiful sister to have for all eternity!

But the greatest joy was yet to come. My Brother turned to me with the most wonderful, gentle look shining from His face and said, "Now I want you to meet the two who were closest to Me when I was on earth—My protector, Saint Joseph, and My own little Mother Mary."

With that we hurried along breathlessly, for both of us could hardly wait for the sheer joy that was in store for us. I can't tell you how fast my heart beat—for suddenly there they were before us—Saint Joseph and our Blessed Mother!

Saint Joseph put his arms around my shoulder, and I knew he was everything and more than I had expected. But this happiness was as nothing compared to what followed when Mary, my Mother, kissed me gently and spoke so quietly to my heart, "Welcome, my son, forever. I see your Brother is taking good care of you. He was at your side through life, and now He'll be at your side in Heaven. Your happiness will be the peace of your Brother close at your side always."

Then it seemed my own mother and father were there and those dearest to me in the love of the Sacred Heart, and all of us just walked, arm in arm, into the flames of God's love—Heart-shaped—and then we seemed to fuse as one in the Beatific Vision of God Himself.

This is what is to be in the home of our Eternal Father with my Brother, Jesus Christ.

God bless and keep you in His Sacred Heart now and forever.

31

Christ Was Truly Human

ALTHOUGH WE ADORE Jesus Christ as the Eternal Son of God, one with His Father in His divine nature, we must never forget that He was also true man. In the world of today, there are some who look upon Him as a vague reality—someone very far away—a sort of an ideal that can't be reached in our modern era of scientific achievement. In this busy, materialistic atmosphere, we seem to forget that the Savior of mankind, the God and Creator of the universe, assumed this same human nature that we possess and was like us in all things, sin alone excepted. Consequently, as man He understands our problems, our trials, our sorrows, our ups and downs of daily living. He was a genuine man, with a human heart, a human mind and soul, and a human body—a complete human nature like our own. The waves and billows of every human emotion passed over his soul just as they do over ours. He wept and rejoiced, grieved and pitied; He was elated and dejected in turns; He was frequently disappointed and saddened and shamed. He was not even immune to temptation, for we know how He was tempted three times by Satan in the desert. And those who say that Christ never laughed have either forgotten or pushed aside the fact that this is a human quality. He could laugh with those who were happy and have a smile for everyone He met, but at the same time He could weep with those who were sad. Like any man He grew weary and tired after a hard day's labor, so much so that He even slept in Peter's little boat in the midst of a violent storm. On occasion He was thirsty and hungry, and He suffered the excruciating pains and torture of His Passion and Crucifixion.

He was a man of unparalleled purity and elevation of character, surpassing in His sublime earnestness the moral grandeur of all other religious teachers, and putting to blush the generally acceptable teachings of such so-called reformers as Confucius, Buddha, Socrates and Plato—and all the other great philosophers of the past. The simple record of three short years of Christ's active life has done more to regenerate and lift mankind to a new level of human living than all the learned dissertations of countless philosophers or moralists. He has set for each one of us a standard of human conduct that's never been equalled.

When He came into this world, He cracked it wide open! Men have loved Him for centuries and still love Him; men have hated Him and still hate Him, but not enough to thwart His influence. He stands at the world's center—the calendar dates from His time. Every word He spoke endures; every step He took is marked; every spot He touched has either inspired a crusade or pilgrimage. He is the founder of Christian civilization, as the name implies. He is at the very heart of the most romantic enterprise ever launched on this earth. Historically He looms so large that His enemies say, "He is too good to be real." His friends say, "He is too good to be invented." When Jesus began to call disciples to Himself, there was an eager response that bespeaks a commanding personality. In a comparatively short time, He had a host of enthusiastic followers and disciples. People who saw Jesus pass by followed Him in crowds.

By gentleness of His character, He could attract little children who clamored all about Him, but at the same time He could excoriate the Pharisees for their hypocrisy. He was all things to all men—the poor and afflicted, the young and the old, despised lepers and men in authority, learned or ignorant, sick or well, the saint or the sinner—all felt perfectly happy and relaxed in His presence. And yet He was unwaveringly resolute in His purpose—He came to carry out His Father's will—and nothing could stop Him. In Him we find courage, charity, tenderness, forgiveness, loyalty, and all other human perfections.

Truly, judging Him as a man amongst men, aside from the fact He was God, and you still have the most outstanding personality in history. For here is God's idea of perfect manhood—manhood without a flaw.

God bless and keep you in His Sacred Heart now and forever.

32

The Positive Approach to Suffering

IT IS TRUE THAT SUFFERING, both mental and physical, has been called a "punishment," but we should clearly understand that it comes into the lives of individuals not necessarily because they themselves have sinned in the past but because of the Original Sin of our first parents. Our intellects are now darkened, our wills weakened, and our bodies subject to all sorts of human frailties, even death itself, as a direct result of this sin that we inherit. Certainly it is not the avenging hand of God, but our own sins and infidelities to Him in the past.

Now that Jesus Christ, the Son of God, has become man, once and for all He has done away with the false notions of suffering. He Himself touched every agony. Now, because of the suffering Christ, the whole Christian world has come to know the beauty and joy and power of sacrifice and suffering in union with Him. This is the positive approach to suffering and gives meaning to it.

The oblation which He made of Himself on the cross and the Christian attitude on suffering and sacrifice have always been closely linked together. Some years ago, a very holy old missionary had to undergo an extremely painful operation, but because it was Good Friday, he absolutely refused to take an anesthetic. "I have my crucifix, and that is enough for me," was all he would say, as he held it tightly in his hand. Throughout the entire operation he suffered in silence, but it was only too evident the heroic price he had to pay. When finally it was all over, he fell back exhausted, and the crucifix that he had clutched so tightly during the entire operation fell from his hand.

It was now bent and twisted—mute testimony of the terrible ordeal he had just undergone.

"Why," you may ask, "did he wish to suffer in this manner? Why did he place himself, as it were, on the altar of sacrifice as an oblation to Almighty God?" I'll tell you why! It was because he had learned the lesson which Jesus Christ came into this world to teach—the lesson of sacrifice at cost to self for the One loved. God's grace had burned into his heart and mind the understanding not only that suffering is a punishment for sin, but also that every quiver of pain endured in this world for His sake is a way of manifesting his loyalty to Him. He deeply realized that there is glory in sacrifice, and to suffer with and for Christ crucified was a special way of proving his intense love for his Savior. Not that pain in itself is of any value, but it is the offering up of it in union with Christ who sanctified suffering by taking it upon Himself.

This does not mean, however, that we must despairingly raise our hands to Heaven and cry out, "If I'm going to get to Heaven, I've got to be glad to suffer!" No one likes pain, even though it will necessarily come upon all of us sooner or later. So, the secret of enduring pain is to supernaturalize it.

Now what a sublime, uplifting motive Christ has brought to poor, suffering humanity! Torn and bleeding and afflicted, now all man has to do is to look to Christ outstretched on the cross. To understand suffering in this way, one must have a strong faith which leads inevitably to a deep abiding friendship with our divine Lord.

God bless and keep you in His Sacred Heart now and forever.

33

The Christ Child and the Poor

THE BIRTH OF JESUS CHRIST, the Eternal Son of God, in the stable of Bethlehem is a joyful mystery clothed in the garment of want, humiliation, and poverty. He came in this way so that once and for all He might do away with the false criterion of the world that a man's worth is dependent on how much of this world's goods he possesses.

Picture for a moment the first Christmas morning. Look into that cave on the outskirts of Bethlehem and behold Him whose tiny hands, though not quite long enough to touch the rough crib in which He lies, hold the reins that guide the planets, the sun, the moon, the stars in their wondrous courses! We see this Infant Child, the newborn King, with His glowing face looking up into His Mother's own, lying there in a manger and wrapped in swaddling clothes. We feel the cold with Him—the icy winds of the wintry night. How we wish we were there, so that we too might pay our homage and adoration as did His first visitors, the poor shepherds from the surrounding hillsides.

Truly, the birth of our Infant Savior in a wretched cave gives us a perfect picture of what love really means: to give up, to sacrifice everything for the one loved. By becoming a helpless baby, Jesus Christ, our God upon whom we depend for every breath we breathe, for every thought that courses through our minds, literally emptied Himself, as Saint Paul says, taking upon Himself the nature of a slave, one of His own creatures. All this because He loves man so much.

This thought of how much our divine Lord loves us by His becoming man was brought home to me recently when I saw a little girl with a pet hamster in her hands. She was lovingly stroking the small animal and cuddling it next to her cheek.

"You love your little pet very much, don't you, Maryanne?" I asked her.

"Oh, yes I do," was her quick reply.

"Would you love it enough to become a little hamster yourself so that you could share its life and be one with it? Would you put aside everything you have—your lovely face and body, your beautiful clothes and playthings, so that you could be just like this little hamster?"

Maryanne was shocked, "Of course not! I would never do that!"

And yet our Loving Savior did far more when He divested Himself of His divinity, as it were, and reduced Himself to the slavery of human nature. For a man to be lowered to the level of a brute animal, he is still on the natural, finite plane, but for God to become man, He had to transcend the infinite, supernatural, uncreated plane of God and lower Himself to our finite, natural level. And this is exactly what He did—and for only one reason, because He loves man so much! By His becoming man in the midst of poverty, humiliations, and sufferings, He has given an example of the only sure way to eternal happiness. He says, "I am the way, the truth, and the life" (Jn 14:6). If I follow Him, He will lead me to certain victory. His way is not the way of the world, and He has proved this by the way He lived His life here on earth.

Now, there is a glory in being poor for Christ's sake. When you cry out, "I don't like poverty," you can pierce right through that abstract noun "poverty" and see the " poor Christ" in the cave of Bethlehem. So too with humiliations. You may say at times, "I don't like humiliations." But now you can see the "humiliated Christ," a tiny baby wrapped in swaddling clothes. So too with suffering. You recoil at having to bear the heavy burden of pain. But now you see the suffering Christ in the manger and later, on the cross, and rejoice to be able to be one with Him in His plan of life.

From a throne of rough boards and a professor's chair of straw, the little King of the universe has come to teach all of us the way to Heaven. His first lesson is that of His unspeakable love for each of us, His creatures. He opens His baby arms to you—thinks of you—speaks of you—prays for you. He teaches you by His living example how to place the right value on all material things of this world and blesses you when, for His dear sake, you are stripped and detached from all created goods so that you may be heart-free to reach the divinity—to be one with Him!

Christ Jesus came to redeem a sin-laden world, not as a man, but as a little baby. He could have come in all the glory of Solomon with banners, shield, and sabers glistening in the sun, but He, the Messiah, the One sent from God, chose to become an infant in order to dispel all fear from your soul. No one fears a child! He comes thus to win your love, your allegiance—to have Him for your little Brother.

He allows each one of us to approach His sacred side, to kiss His baby hands and feet, and peer into that baby Sacred Heart! What confidence does He not inspire!

Can He refuse you anything if you come to Him with a heart full of love? Place that heart of yours at the foot of the crib today! And if your heart is sorrowful, He will warm it at the flame of Love; if life is lonely, He will be your ever-present Companion, your unchangeable Friend; if you are poor, He will enrich you with everlasting treasures; and if hope is dark, He will be the light of Bethlehem shining over your night and guiding you to the ever-peaceful pastures of paradise.

God bless and keep you in His Sacred Heart now and forever.

34

Have You Found Jesus?

THE STORY IS TOLD of a dramatic young preacher who had been striving for some time to arouse a renewal of faith in the minds and hearts of his listeners and to give them a better understanding of the love of Jesus Christ and the intimate role He should play in their personal lives. At the conclusion of his rather lengthy sermon, he pointed his finger at certain individuals in the congregation and enthusiastically asked the question, "Have you found Jesus?" The response was immediate, "Yes, I've found Jesus!" And to another, "Have you found Jesus?" "Yes, I've found Jesus!" And to another, "Have you found Jesus?" "Yes, I've found Jesus!"

Then he turned to a little boy sitting wide-eyed before him and asked the same question, "Have you found Jesus?" The youngster looked up and said, "I didn't know He was lost."

No truer statement could have been made. It is not Jesus that is lost in our personal lives, but it is we who lose Him by our being too wrapped up and absorbed in the material passing things and pleasures of time and the world to find Him.

Saint John, the Beloved Disciple, tells us how we are to find Him and become aware of His infinite, eternal love for each one of us. In one of his letters to the early Christians, he wrote, "God's love was revealed in our midst; He sent His only Son to the world that we might have life through Him. Love, then, consists in this: not that we have loved God, but that He has loved us and sent His Son as an offering for our sins" (1Jn 4:9–10).

Within this question of Saint John lies a statement, flattering to us and deeply profound for each one of us personally. If we truly grasp what it offers, we will begin to make that response to the love of God, which is the only kind He wants from us, the only kind that will be valuable and permanent.

God has "first loved us." God does not respond to a plea from us or to a need He sees we have. His love for us is a spontaneous love, rising from within Himself and born, amazingly enough, of real affection for us.

It is only someone hardened from hate or prejudiced by a contrary love who cannot return love like that of God's. When we are finally able to appreciate God's love, we cannot help but feel it drain all hatred and hardness out of us. When Jesus Christ in His humanity spoke, only those whose hearts were full of hate, or full of a baser, unworthy love against Him, were unmoved. Those who were of good will and open to His all-compelling influence were swept up into the searing flames of His love.

God, the Creator, generally spoke to the Jews of Himself as someone who had done something for them. He created them after His own image to share in His eternal love if they would but let Him. He led them from the land of bondage under His great prophet, Moses. He gave prosperity to the kingdom of David and constantly watched over and protected the chosen race from whom would come the Messiah, man's Redeemer. And Christ Himself let all those with whom He dealt feel the impact of His love, not so much in the lessons He taught, but in the works He did for them. When the disciples of Saint John the Baptist asked Jesus if He were the one to come or should they look for another, He replied, "Go back and report to John what you hear and see: the blind recover their sight, cripples walk, lepers are cured, the deaf hear, dead men are raised to life, and the poor have the good news preached to them" (Lk 7:22).

How can we personally feel this love of Christ right now? Primarily by imitating and following the example of loving our fellow man by exchanging love with each other. This is brought about not by studying it, but by practicing it: not in words only, but in action. We must be willing to share with others our most precious earthly possessions as well as, and even more importantly, our inmost spiritual treasures of thoughtful appreciation and generous love, even though such a course of action may demand complete sacrifice on our part. But love is sacrifice, as Christ proved. Only when men feel "how good it is to dwell together" will they be won to Christianity.

So if we really want to find Jesus, we must be willing to listen to His teachings and put them into action. "You shall love the Lord your God with all your heart, with all your soul, with all your mind, and with all your strength . . . And you shall love your neighbor as yourself" (Mt 22:37.–39).

God bless and keep you in His Sacred Heart now and forever.

35

The Arms of Christ

RECENTLY, I HAD A VERY UNUSUAL and happy experience when I visited the home of a young married couple with three little children, one a baby in the crib. As I entered their home, they ushered me into the parlor, and there on the wall was a most unusual picture—if you could call it that. Actually it was a block of wood about a foot square. On this block was the image of Christ as though hanging on a cross, but there wasn't any cross. The strange and rather shocking part of this image of Christ was that He didn't have any arms.

I asked the young couple why they had such a grotesque image of our Savior hanging on a block of wood in their parlor, and this was their answer. "Well, you see Father, we want to be the arms of Christ, and this reminds us constantly that He is working and breathing and living through us. We supply His arms."

Inspired by these words of this fine young couple, I thought this was such a wonderful answer to my question that I decided then and there to write this talk and to make this meaningful idea of being Christ's arms an essential part of my preaching and teaching the Word of God.

Yes, we are Christ's arms and legs and heart and mind. All that we do is Jesus Christ doing it in and through us. We today are the saviors of the world by letting Christ take over our humanity and work in and through us. He could have saved the world alone, but instead He lets us help Him as we continue reliving His Mystical Humanity through us. The historical Christ died and was buried in His own Humanity, but the resurrected Christ lives on in other willing humanities in every era of time.

The Second Vatican Council reiterates the words of Saint Paul who cried out in ecstasy, "I live, now not I, but Christ lives in me" (Gal

2:20), when it expressed this same beautiful, inspiring way of life in its treatise on the Church in the Modern World (Gaudium et Spes)[1]. Here, it explains in explicit words the definite role the lay people in their state of life are to play in carrying out the divine plan of Jesus Christ for the salvation of souls.

> Each individual layman must stand before the world as a witness to the Resurrection and life of the Lord Jesus and as a sign that God lives. As a body and individually, the laity must do their part to nourish the work with spiritual fruits and to spread abroad in it that spirit by which are animated those poor, meek, and peacemaking men whom the Lord in the gospel calls blessed. In a word, what the soul is to the body, let Christians be to the world. (LG 38)

> The lay apostolate, however, is a participation in the saving mission of the Church itself. Through their baptism and confirmation, all are commissioned to that apostolate by the Lord Himself. Moreover, through the sacraments, especially the Holy Eucharist, there is communicated and nourished that charity toward God and man which is the soul of the entire apostolate. No, the laity, are called in a special way to make the Church present and operative in those places and circumstances where only through them can she become the salt of the earth. (LG 33)

> To those, therefore, who believe in divine love, He gives assurance that the way of love lies open to all men and that the effort to establish a universal brotherhood is not a hopeless one. He cautions them at the same time that this love is not something to be reserved for important matters, but must be pursued chiefly in the ordinary circumstances of life. (GS 38)

> We do not know the time for the consummation of the earth and of humanity. Nor do we know how all things will be transformed. As deformed by sin, the shape of this world will pass away. But we

---

1   Ed. Note: Fr. Parrish cites here both Gaudium et Spes and the Dogmatic Constitution on the Church (Lumen Gentium).

are taught that God is preparing a new dwelling place and a new earth where justice will abide, and whose blessedness will answer and surpass all the longings of peace which spring up in the human heart. (GS 39)

God bless and keep you in His Sacred Heart now and forever.

36

Suffering Crosses in Imitation of Him

THE WOMAN I WAS VISITING in the hospital knew she was slowly dying with an incurable disease and that her days were numbered. Lines of pain in her face spoke even more expressively how willingly she accepted her last bitter agony in union with our divine Savior, Jesus Christ, in His Passion.

"I can help Jesus carry His cross," she whispered, "but really when you come right down to it, all I'm carrying is but a tiny splinter of His cross He lovingly shares with me."

Isn't it true we all have to suffer one way or another here on earth! Sorrow and suffering are intimate companions at every step of the way to all of us. Now, when the shadow of the cross darkens our path, there are two ways to look at it: we may raise our heads to question God's justice and refuse to accept the comfort of the suffering Savior, or we may take this suffering gratefully to our hearts, as this woman did, as a pure proof of Christ's love for us—the same type of love He had for those who were nearest and dearest to those He loved most! What heartrending anguish that dearest of all creatures to Him, His own precious Blessed Mother, had to endure! Recall the bitter suffering and intense mental anguish of His foster-father, Saint Joseph; the heroic martyrdom of Saint John the Baptist; the many trials, difficulties, and final suffering and death of His chosen followers, the apostles; and on down through the centuries we see that those who followed Christ most closely were always given the cross to bear. Think of the martyrs, confessors, mothers and fathers and virgins who have been living holocausts on the altar of suffering. Surely these must be a sign of intimate union between Christ and those whom He especially loves.

Saint Paul, who suffered indescribable torments during his constant zealous preaching of Christ and Christ crucified, and who was finally beheaded, realized that to suffer with and for Christ was a special way of proving his intense love for his Savior. He knew that it is the gift of oneself that matters—nothing else—in the eyes of his crucified Christ—the gift of the human heart—its homage, its reverence, its service, the outpouring of itself in whatever condition it might be placed, even the giving of life itself, whether that life is destined to live on or is demanded as a present sacrifice. "Christ loved me, and gave Himself for me," He cried out, dumbfounded at God's generosity, and he answers with a heart bursting to make a return of love. "I am sure that neither death nor life, nor angels nor principalities, nor powers, nor things present nor things to come, nor might nor height, nor depth, nor any other creature shall be able to separate me from the love of God, which is in Christ Jesus our Lord" (Rom 8:38–39).

He had learned the lesson well that true love impels to love—and love impels to sacrifice for the beloved. Yes, love of suffering and even the acceptance of suffering demands great courage. But if you would love Him well and deeply you must be prepared, like Saint Paul, to lay down your life for your Friend and, if need be, to lay down anything that is of less moment than life.

Think how much easier the sick in the hospitals throughout the world could bear their sufferings if they would only look to Christ for their inspiration and receive everything as coming from His hands for their sanctification. How much easier to accept the cross in this manner, for He Himself said, "My yoke is sweet and my burden light" (Mt 11:30). But it is only sweet and light when we let Him place that yoke across our shoulders with His gentle hand, for then it is carried by two—Christ and me.

We know from our own experience that it is easier to accept medicine from the hand of one we love, from our own mother, for example, rather than anyone else. So, too, is it easier to accept our sufferings—and we'll always have them—from the hand of Christ, the One whom we love and who loves us more than anyone else in the world.

Everyone has to suffer. Why not, therefore, accept suffering in this way—glorify pain in union with Christ in suffering. The two thieves hanging on crosses on either side of our Savior both suffered the same pains. The one on the left turned his gaze away from Christ and blasphemed Him, but the one on the right turned his gaze toward Christ, suffered with Christ and for Him, and consequently won Heaven. Simon, the Cyrenean, helped our Lord to carry His cross ever so little. Christ could have borne it alone, but because Simon shared Christ's cross with Him in some slight degree, his name has gone down in the annals of history as the one who helped Jesus to bear His cross. Veronica tried to lighten His sufferings by wiping the dirt and blood and spittle from His face and eyes, and she was rewarded with a gift beyond all compare—the imprint of Christ's face in her veil.

The saints of God knew the strength and power in the cross of Jesus Christ. Have we learned this lesson? In times of loneliness, sorrow, sufferings, take your crucifix in your hand, and draw strength from Christ's sufferings. In the cross is our strength—our hope—our salvation. By carrying the cross with Christ, we shall also share in His crown of glory.

God bless and keep you in His Sacred Heart now and forever.

37

The Crucified and Risen Christ

LIFE WITHOUT LOVE IS EMPTY! Love without sacrifice has no meaning! Jesus Christ crucified on the cross and risen from the dead is love personified. His is the story of a God who loves man to passion and death, even to the folly of the cross: who sacrificed His own life that man might live. In His bitter Passion, He touched every problem that afflicts our troubled lives, knew every pang of loss and grief and suffering, experienced every agony. He didn't have to suffer so intensely to redeem man. One drop of His Precious Blood would have been more than enough. But He chose to tread the wine press of agony and crucifixion for one reason only, and that is because He loves each one of us personally to an infinite degree. Yes, God could have saved us in many ways, but He could not have saved us unless He loved us. Saint Paul made it very personal when he said "He loved me, and delivered Himself up for me" (Gal 2:20). I personally am the one whom Christ loves and died for.

Some may ask, "Why could He not have loved us and redeemed us without death? Again the only answer to this question is to repeat over and over again—the death of Jesus Christ reveals to us how absolutely conditionless God's love is for man. We were saved, not by the physical death of Jesus, but by the infinite love of a God Who did not count death too high a price to pay. In dying, Jesus was obedient to His Eternal Father, even to the pouring out of His life's blood like water. "Greater love than this no man has, that he be willing to die for his friend" (Jn 5–13). And this is exactly what the Son of God did to prove His love.

But love is of two! On our part we must never forget that love will always be asked of us in return. The cross reveals that this love is one that is also completely sacrificial in its nature, both towards God and our neighbor. And we, too, must be willing to make an oblation of ourselves for our Friend—a constant dying to self that He might live within us.

Perhaps this might be better understood it I told you of a very consoling thought that has helped me to understand this sacrificial union between yourself and Christ. Did it ever occur to you that the only thing our divine Lord ever became attached to was the wood of the cross? So, if we become the wood of the cross we let Him become so attached to us that there will never be any separation. Remember He said that if He were lifted up, He would draw all things to Himself. If He be lifted up through the divine indwelling on the wood in us, He will draw all things through us to Himself.

We know that He had to carry the wood of the cross—and He may have to carry us also. He will "take hold," if we just become like the wood in His arms—that complete limpness in letting Him pick us up and carry us. It sort of comes down to that absolute trust in Him, confident that He can carry the burden, and that without Him we are absolutely helpless, like wood lying along the roadway of life.

This is a sort of abandonment to His Will, knowing that whatever way He carries the wood—on His shoulder, under His arm, at His side near His Heart, or dragging it behind Him—is the best way for us to reach the top of the mountain, where there will take place the final and irrevocable attachment when the nails pierce through His living flesh and join us to Him in an inseparable bond of love. This will be our death to self that He might be resurrected in us. He died on the wood of the cross and was buried, but we know He rose from the dead on the third day and continues His resurrected life in all who will let Him. Truly, if the death of Jesus on the summit of Golgotha is a revelation of His infinite love, the Resurrection is a summons to deeper faith in His living Presence within us and a stronger hope of eternal oneness with Him forever in Heaven.

I would like to close now with the words of the poem "God and Pain."

The cry of earth's anguish went up to God—"Lord, take away pain—
the shadow that darkens the world Thou hast made, the close-coiling

chain that strangles the heart: the burden that weighs on wings that would soar. Lord, take away pain from the world Thou hast made that it love Thee the more!"

Then answerest the Lord to the world He had made, "Shall I take away pain? And with it the power of the soul to endure, made strong by the strain? Shall I take away pity that knits heart to heart, and sacrifice high? Will ye lose all your heroes who lift from the flame white brows to the sky? Shall I take away love that redeems with a price, and smiles through the loss? Can ye spare from the lives that would climb unto

Mine—the Christ on His Cross?"

God bless and keep you in His Sacred Heart now and forever.

38

The Meaning of the Resurrection

ONE TIME A YOUNG MAN came to a learned scholar and asked him the question, "How can I start my own religion?" The wise man answered, "Go get yourself killed and then rise from the dead."

Where in the history of the world has anyone dared to do what Jesus Christ did? In my meditation, I can hear Him say, "Kill Me, and as sure as you kill Me, I'll arise from the dead and confound the world. Crucify Me; drive a spear into My Heart, and you will prove that I am truly the Son of God—for I will rise from the dead on the third day, as I promised."

Christ died, yes, but He also rose from the dead, glorious and immortal—rose by His own power, and by so doing proved His message was true: that He was the Son of God, sent from His Eternal Father to teach mankind how to get to Heaven. Yes, Christ died, and if He had stayed buried in the tomb there would be no more to say, but Christ rose, and by His Resurrection we have the assurance of our own resurrection unto life everlasting. No wonder Saint Paul exclaimed, "If Christ has not been raised, your faith is vain" (1 Cor 17).

Think what it means to bring oneself back to life by one's own power! Can anyone else but God perform such a miracle of miracles? Only He is the Master over life and death!

Yet Christ stands—we can picture Him in His glorified Humanity above an empty tomb—His face shining as the sun, His garments white as snow, a conqueror of death, a victor over suffering and sin—not for Himself, but for us. "I am," He gently assures us, as He did to Martha at the death of her brother Lazarus, "the Resurrection and the life. Whoever believes in Me will live, even though he dies; and whoever lives and believes in Me will never die" (Jn 11:25–26).

The Resurrection teaches that out of fear can come courage; out of anxiety can come peace. Physical pain is a currency that can buy happiness. The Resurrection teaches us that there is a blessedness in poverty and mercy, in suffering and peacemaking—in carrying the cross after Christ, for we know that He fought for the kingdom of Heaven and He brings it to those whom He loves. Here is the glorified Humanity of the Savior of the world communicating to men—to His Mystical Body, the Church—His most precious gift: a newness of life, a oneness with Him in His own divine life.

And so real is this supernatural life of Christ that it is said to be more real than our own natural life. "It is no longer I that live," cried out Saint Paul, enraptured with the awesomeness of Christ's life dwelling in his soul, "but Christ lives in me" (Gal 2:20).

Now there is nothing to fear in the whole world. With this divine life to strengthen and console us, there can never again be real sadness in our lives. Sorrow and suffering? Yes. For Christ Himself predicted this in His own life: "the Son of man must suffer greatly and be rejected by the elders, the chief priest and the scribes, and be put to death, and rise after three days" (Mk 9:31). Work and weariness? Yes. Persecution and martyrdom? Yes. But, sadness, despair, discouragement, fear? Never! Once the truth of the Resurrection sinks deep into our hearts and that we have the very life of God to strengthen us, there can be no room for anything but peace, joy, and happiness.

The Risen Savior summons before Him each suffering soul in all generations and shows each of these His glorified wounds. In my prayerful imagination I see the risen Savior as He summons before Him every suffering soul in all generations and shows each of these His glorified Wounds. In effect He reassures each one on his bed of pain, "It was worth it!" He consoles each broken heart, "It's worth it all." He lifts each agonizing face from its pillow of suffering and opens the eyes of the blind so that not one may be deprived of the inspiring vision of His Wounds in glory. He listens to every single complaint uttered in agony of sickness and sorrow. To the crippled and paralyzed He says, "Put your finger here in the Wounds of My hands and feet, and see how they shine now in glory." To the broken-hearted and discouraged He beckons, "Put your hand in My side—and now share a foretaste of your own glory with Me." Perhaps the agonizing sufferer may cry out, "It's too much, Lord, I just can't bear it any longer." But the risen Savior answers, "Look, My child, at My Wounds—put your hand in My side, your finger in My hands, See how the Wounds shine. It is all worth it. Courage, My friend, your present suffering will one day be a crown of glory for you—and even now you have My divine life to sustain you." To each He whispers the mystery of His own suffering—and of the glory that is to come for those who take up their cross and follow after Him.

Truly, our life here on earth is so like the Holy Sacrifice of the Mass—a constant renewal of the Passion and death of Christ—but it is also a blending of His glorious Resurrection unto everlasting glory with Him in Heaven.

God bless and keep you in His Sacred Heart now and forever.

39

Crowning the Man of Sorrows

OUR SAVIOR, JESUS CHRIST, having endured the tortures of His agony in the garden; condemned in the name of politics by Annas, the high priest; laughed to scorn and treated as a fool by the sensuous Herod; and unjustly judged in the name of religion by Caiaphas, was then turned over to the sadistic guards to pass the night in a whirlwind of humiliation.

And so early in the morning, He is rushed to the hall of Pontius Pilate, the Roman governor, who—knowing Christ to be innocent—tries every available evasion to release Him, first sending Him to Herod when he heard that he was a Galilean, and on second investigation, finding Christ still not guilty, compromiser that he was, delivers Him to the brutal soldiers to be scourged then releases Barabbas, a criminal, in place of Christ. Finally, in desperation, Pilate washes his hands and declares, "I am innocent of the blood of this just man" (Mt 27:24). Nevertheless, he delivers Him to the Roman soldiers to be crucified.

Saint Matthew tells us the story: "Then the soldiers of the governor taking Jesus into the hall, gathered together unto Him the whole band, and stripping Him they put a scarlet cloak about Him. And plaiting a crown of thorns, they put it upon His head and a reed in His Hand. And bowing the knee before Him, they mocked Him saying, 'Hail, King of the Jews.' And spitting upon Him they took the reed, and struck His head, and after that they mocked Him" (Mt 27:31).

In the garden His Father had given Him a chalice to drink—this seems to be the nauseating part of the draft, but all motivated by the driving force of me. I'm the one Saint Paul had in mind when he wrote, "He loved me and delivered Himself for me."

These soldiers look on His face—so calm and clean! Then spit on it—that's the thing to do! He has no right to be straight! He is so silent in His sufferings! Then strike Him across the mouth until He breaks that silence! His eyes look so kindly and benevolently at them! Then dodge the reproach that's in those eyes! Blindfold Him! He said He loves God! Then blaspheme God! He is so obviously pure! Then say things that will shock Him! Curse God!

He claimed to be king! Then crown Him! Give Him a diadem worthy of such a king—a crown of thorns! Drive them deeply into His head! Here's His scepter—a reed! Strike Him hard across the head with it—that'll show how much power He has! So they did—they played with God! Tear the clothes from off His bleeding shoulders and cover Him with a cast-off soldier's cloak for His royal robe! He needs a throne—here, shove Him up on this broken pillar—that's good enough for Him! Let's all get a good stomach full of laughter out of Jesus of Nazareth!

What a horrible blasphemy to heap upon the very God who created them! Here is the Messiah, the long expected of nations, the Redeemer, and yet He is mocked as a fool! Here is the Creator of the whole universe, and yet His creatures crown Him with a diadem of shame, and the earth He brought into existence brings forth but thorns, thistles, and a reed for Him!

Why this defiling suffering? Why this abuse? Why this crowning of thorns? There is only one answer. These drops of blood flowing down His face, these deep gashes caused by the thorns encircling His head like a basket speak by silence more eloquently than words of the divine love that burns in His Heart for each one of us. He suffered all this because He was taking my place, because He knew I could never stand it. Every evil thought of mine presses the thorns deeper into His head; every sinful word is another smashing blow across His lips; every evil thing I look upon is spittle in His eyes; every impurity is another lash upon His back! Yes, He is a king, but not of this world of passing glory. He rejected a crown of gold and the rich robes of royalty to accept instead a crown of thorns and the purple rags of mockery and scorn for our sake, because He wanted us to know the real value of our eternal kingship with Him in His Heavenly kingdom where there will be no end.

He would rather be a fool in the eyes of men than a king of this world so fleeting. He is strong in His immortal glory in Heaven, because of His mortal wounds on earth. How they shine now! His conquering weapons—silence and tears! The royal purple—His Sacred Humanity dyed in His own crimson blood! The crown—His prickly diadem of aching pain! His scepter—the devastating power of infinite love!

This is a picture of the Man of Sorrows. This is the conqueror of men's hearts! This is my leader—the only One who will lead me on to certain victory, if I but let Him have His way with me.

God bless and keep you in His Sacred Heart now and forever.

40

The Crown of Eternal Life

THE GREATEST TEACHER of all mankind, Jesus Christ, has told us over and over again to keep our hearts and minds centered always on what God, our Heavenly Father, has in store for those that love and serve Him here on earth. "Do not lay up for yourselves treasures on earth," He says, "where rust and moth consume, and where thieves break in and steal; but lay up for yourselves treasures in Heaven, where neither rust nor moth consumes, nor thieves break in and steal. For where your treasure is, there also will your heart be" (Mt 6:19–21).

This positive teaching of Christ of striving to be aware of the shortness of our earthly existence with all its difficulties and the eternity of forever in perfect happiness with our Father in Heaven is a wonderful, steadying way of keeping a deep-down peace in our soul, even in the midst of the most devastating and disconcerting trials. With perfect confidence in God and His infinite love and watchfulness over us, knowing that He will be there constantly at our side every moment of our earthly life and waiting for us on the other side is a sure way of keeping spiritual balance and true happiness.

To one who truly believes in these promises of our divine Savior, in whom there is this hope of a blessed resurrection, life is not taken away; it is but changed to an infinitely happier place with our Creator forever. And when the home of this earthly sojourn is dissolved, an eternal dwelling place is being prepared in Heaven.

Since we all have to carry our cross in one way or another as a result of Original Sin, this is why our divine Savior holds out to us the happy prospect of a crown of glory as our everlasting reward. It is consoling to know that every spasm of pain will have its recompense in joy. Jesus

Christ, standing above the empty tomb glorious and immortal with His countenance shining as the sun, teaches this lesson more eloquently than any words of mine. In my own reflective prayer, I can almost hear Him say to each one agonizing on his bed of pain, "Be comforted, child; look how My wounds shine in glory now, and so will yours. Take comfort—for you, too, will walk again in the halls of Heaven." To all who tread the wine-press of suffering be what it may—physical or mental, emotional or spiritual—He reassures each one with His comforting words, "Friend, it's worth it all. Have confidence in Me and know that very soon I will wipe away all tears from your eyes, and death shall be no more, nor mourning nor crying nor sorrow."

So do not lose heart when crosses seem almost beyond human strength to endure. Look up to the smiling, glorious face of Christ our Lord with His arms outstretched toward you and hear Him say, "Remember, I'm here waiting for you in Heaven. Unite that cross with Mine on your via dolorosa to Calvary's heights, and you will surely rise with Me in glory forever."

I can't help but think of Nancy Hamilton, the a little girl who suffered through innumerable severe operations from infancy because of an incurable disease she had incurred. I had the happiness of bringing our divine Savior to her when she made her First Holy Communion in Saint John's Hospital in California. Later, both her legs had to be amputated, but the inner peace and love of Jesus in her soul radiated through her beautiful face as she brought cheer and happiness to the other patients. When asked what philosophy of life she lived by to be so cheerful in the midst of such suffering, she unhesitatingly replied, "I don't look down! I look up—up to God, and God helps me."

It wasn't long after this that her same loving God whom she had looked up to every moment of her life called her home to be happy with Him forever in Heaven. At that time, her mother wrote this beautiful poem titled, "New Angel," which I would like to share with you:

Hold her gently, Jesus; she was very tired today.
She tried so hard to hide the pain, and keep the tears away.
You know how much she suffered, Lord,
Yet loved You all the while.
You know how many heartaches were hidden in a smile.

So hold her gently, Jesus, and I am sure You'll say,
"The Cross she bore so patiently
Became her Crown today."

May the cross that you carry so bravely today become your crown
of glory also in Heaven tomorrow, whenever that may be.

God bless and keep you in His Sacred Heart now and forever.

41

The Key to Success in Prayer

"GOD NEVER ANSWERS MY PRAYERS, Father. As far as I can make out, when I try to speak to God, it is like talking to a blank wall. I don't know; I'm beginning to think God has too many things to do and to take care of that He just doesn't have time to listen to me, and sometimes I really don't blame Him very much. After all, who am I to ask God to help me—I've never done very much for Him. But, really, Father, I would like to know, how does one have success in prayer?"

Frequently, priests do hear such complaints and questions on the subject of prayer. How to get in contact with God? Does God really hear our prayers? Is there any secret way of meeting success, a sort of supernatural formula that all but impels God to listen, some kind of magic key that opens up the heavenly vistas leading to the eternal treasure vaults, where God stores up His gifts for men and then suddenly pours them out on those chosen esoteric few who happen to possess the key?

Yes: God, being infinite, does listen to every sincere man's prayer, whether he be rich or poor, old or young, beautiful or not. And we also know that no one is too unimportant for God to hear and take care of, if such is the best for him in the light of eternity for his soul's salvation.

Our Lord Himself exhorted us to pray, and pray often, and not to hesitate to ask for anything: "If you ask the Father anything in My Name He will give it to you. Ask and it shall be given to you; seek and you shall find; knock and it shall be opened unto you. Hitherto you have not asked anything in My Name. Ask and you shall receive that your joy may be full" (Mt 7:7–8). Yes, truly, if we have faith, we can move mountains.

Here is the key; here is the formula enunciated by Christ Himself. If we are to be successful in prayer—then do all in His Name and with His divine power dwelling within our souls through grace. Certainly, if we expect God to answer our prayer, first of all we should be God's friends. It doesn't seem to be quite right to be slapping God with one hand by offending Him, and with the other reaching up with open palm begging His special help or condescension. That's the first essential. If you want to be successful in prayer, be sure that you are God's friend in sanctifying grace; get close to His Sacred Heart by frequent Holy Communion, and make sure that your whole day is a living consecration to God as a way of life by offering up everything you do or think or say in your daily Morning Offering.

Then, also remember that God may have ideas other than what you think are best for you. After all, you cannot see very far and what you are asking for may not be for your eternal good. If God were to answer your prayer in precisely the way you are demanding for yourself, who knows the difficulties, disappointments, and sorrows for many that may ensue, even the loss of souls. In other words, God looks at all things down the long, long ages of eternity, and He knows what is best in that light—and you don't. Actually, as time goes on, I'm sure that all of us can understand how good God has been to us in not always granting what we judge to be for our personal advantage at the time.

"God," we cry out, "take away this pain, this sorrow, this suffering, and I'll love You the more for it." Please God, spare my child." "Oh, don't let him die, God, he's all I've got." "This cross is too heavy, and I just can't carry it any longer." "God, what am I going to do, I'm so burdened with debts, won't You help me?"

And on and on men and women plead to God in endless cries and, at times, seemingly to no avail. Yet, if God answered their prayer in the way they want, they would not have the opportunity to sanctify themselves, or to prepare to die well, or so to live on earth that it does not take their gaze away from their eternal home in Heaven.

So, if one wants to succeed in prayer, always remember that God knows best—and we must not try to conform God's will to ours, but ours to His. The most perfect prayer of petition that was ever uttered here on earth fell from the lips of Jesus Christ Himself in the agony of the garden. When He was all but overwhelmed at the ordeal He had to face the next day—the bloody scourging at the pillar, the crowning with thorns, the horrible crucifixion—from a human point of view, He shrunk away in terror. Added to this were all the sins of mankind, past, present, and future, that pressed upon Him and all but nauseated Him with the fetid odor of moral corruption. Yet, even in the midst of all this, when He called upon His Heavenly Father to take away the chalice, He quickly added, "but not My will, but Thine be done" (Mt 26:42). Here was the perfect prayer—and yet Christ still had to undergo His bitter Passion and death to carry out the will of His Eternal Father. The timeworn expression in time of sorrow, "God knows best," is still just as true today as it ever was.

God bless and keep you in His Sacred Heart now and forever.

42

Give Us This Day Our Daily Bread

WHAT A HAPPY PHILOSOPHY OF LIFE, to take each day as it comes—to measure earthly values in the light of eternity, and strive to look at all things in the way God Himself looks at them. I am sure this is what our divine Savior had in mind when He told His apostles to say "Give us this day our daily bread" (Lk 11:3).

Such an outlook on life and its daily needs is a great help to keep that deep-down peace of soul which is so necessary if we are to advance in our love for God. It is a certain strong trust in His divine Providence that all will turn out for the best in His eyes if we but daily keep up our confidence in His omnipotent watchfulness over us.

I recall the old gentleman who told me about a year before he died that this was his philosophy of life. As he prayed the words, "Give us this day our daily bread," he would take that particular day and look at it as though it were the last he was going to live. "I have been suffering from angina pectoris for some years," he told me, "and expect to die at any moment, but," he quickly added, "I don't worry in the least, because I have a definite philosophy of life which I learned long, long ago, even before I was sick—and this is it. I always live each day as though it were the moment of eternity for me—as though God might call me to Himself today. And you know, I always have a song in my heart that God will take care of me. In fact, with this outlook, it's easy for me to suffer these constant headaches. When it's hard for me to get up to go to daily Holy Mass, and Holy Communion too, I reflect that this day is the most important day of my life—and it may be my last. I say to myself, "What would I want to do if I were to die today?" And, honestly, Father, it does make it a lot easier to do the better thing."

I asked him, "Don't you find living like this from day to day rather difficult and trying at times?"

"Well, Father," he replied, "If I didn't have my Faith, I don't know what I would do. But as it is, I accept all from His hands and know that whatever He sends me is for the best in His eyes. He has His own plans, and I live day by day as though He were going to call me on that day." And that's exactly how he died—and I'm sure the Just Judge was more than ordinarily pleased with his daily prayer.

Then I remember the other man of middle age, a doctor, but also suffering continually from a serious heart condition. Daily he would attend two and three Masses and receive Holy Communion, even though it demanded a superhuman effort for him to do so. When his own doctor told him he would have to take it easy and not strain his heart by going so often to Church, his reply was simple but deeply meaningful, "If I'm going to die, I would rather die on my way to meeting Jesus, or on my return home from just having received Him in Holy Communion."

The words "Give us this day our daily bread" meant far more to him than life itself, for he left this life as he died: in the embrace of Jesus, his King, just having received Him in the Bread of Eternal Life that very morning.

When will we ever learn this lesson? If we lived day by day as though it were our last, accepting everything as coming from His hands, how much easier it would be to bear up under our cross of suffering, our lonely hours—the constant struggle to be good! Like a little child being cared for by his father and mother, we too must rest day by day on God's divine Providence. Be not troubled about the morrow, for our Father in Heaven takes thought of it for us—foresees everything, arranges everything.

Of course, this does not mean that we shouldn't have a certain prudent provision for the future, but God does not wish us to be overanxious about difficulties and evils that may never occur. Is He not right? How true it is that the greater part of mankind are made more wretched on account of their foolish worries about the future than by what they suffer in the present. The cares that undermine our health, both of body and mind, will not avert the accidents and sufferings, the separations and sorrows which all of us see looming in the indefinite future. God alone has the power to preserve us from evil—and He will, if we but trust Him. Say often, "Sacred Heart of Jesus, I place my trust in You."

God bless and keep you in His Sacred Heart now and forever.

43

Our Divine Model in Prayer

OUR DIVINE SAVIOR JESUS CHRIST is the perfect model of how to pray, for His life was one of continual prayer—of constant union with His Eternal Father. Prayer was His very food and drink, and every moment of His life was the perfection of this union.

From our earliest days of childhood, we learned that prayer was the lifting of our minds and hearts to God. Was there anyone who carried this out more effectively than did the divine Master Himself? From the first breath He took as a little infant lying in the manger (for being God He could pray) until His dying breath on the cross, "Father, into Thy hands, I commend My Spirit" (Lk 23:46), His mind and heart were one with His Father's.

As a young boy at Nazareth and during all the long years of His hidden life, He teaches us how to pray by His willingness to submit to the ordinary routine of daily living without external distractions to take our minds away from important things. These days, though humdrum and seemingly unimportant, were considered by His Eternal Father to be the best days of His life. Why? Because they were days of constant awareness of His Father's presence, even in the midst of apparently unimportant activities. He sanctified every action, every thought, every breath by a willing submission, obedience, and resignation to whatever came His way. For He knew all the while that He was perfectly fulfilling God's will in everything. Daily we can almost hear Him say His Morning Offering, "My Father in Heaven, take this day with all its joys and sufferings, its pains and sorrows. May all be to Your glory and the salvation of those whom You have sent Me to redeem, and may My daily offering lift each one up to a participation in Your divinity."

As we study Him further, we find that before He started out in His public life where He would be rubbing shoulders with all sorts of people, He took "time out" to spend forty days of prayer and sacrifice in the desert. Here was the Son of God Himself—and He teaches us how necessary it is to build up the interior life before launching out on any undertaking, if we expect to be strong enough to overcome the temptations of evil and the attraction of the world and all its pleasures. Strength from this kind of prayer is of the utmost importance in our daily struggle to keep our souls in His love. If we are to meet the hardships of daily living in the midst of a world that's pretty materialistic; if we are to fight off and conquer the allurements of this fallen human nature of ours, we, too, must fire up this mind and heart of ours with a willingness to give time to this prayer of sacrifice and silence, like the divine Master in the desert. If He thought it was so important, who are we to say, "It's all right for you, Jesus Christ, to pray in this manner, but not for me! I don't need it!" He prayed to show us how important it is to conquer self first before attempting to save others.

We read in the Gospel account of His life how before every undertaking He would betake Himself to prayer and ask His Father's blessing upon it. At times, too, He would spend the whole night in prayer, even though He had spent the day in preaching and laboring among the people. Certainly no one can ever say that Jesus Christ in His human nature never taught by word and example—this latter being a far more eloquent lesson—the necessity of prayer in our daily living.

But perhaps the greatest lesson of all that He taught was the one we learn from His bitter Passion and death, particularly His prayer in the agony in the garden. Here we find the Son of God in utter anguish as the full impact of sin strikes upon His human soul. Generation after generation of the vilest kinds of evil, past, present, and future, fairly nauseate Him as the corrupt legions of men and women of all centuries drown Him with the fetid odor of sin, until He is a worm and no man. No wonder He cries out, "Father, if it be possible, let this chalice pass from me." But he quickly added, "Not My will, but Thine be done" (Mt 26:42). This is the perfect prayer. Jesus Christ recognized the importance of submission, even though it meant suffering, bitterness, and death. But He also knew that it would mean the redemption of mankind and the glory of the Resurrection.

We don't always understand what God has in mind for us, for His ways are not always our ways. But we also know His ways are the best in the light of eternity. To pray like this after the example of the greatest model of all prayer, Jesus Christ Himself, may lead us to passion and death, but it will also lead to the glory of eternal happiness with Him forever.

God bless and keep you in His Sacred Heart now and forever.

44

Prayer and Freedom

DID IT EVER OCCUR TO YOU that prayer is a human act involving the intellect and free will? One cannot pray unless he is intelligent enough to acknowledge his dependence on God, freely turn to Him, and be willing to do what is pleasing to Him. A truly mature individual sees the need of prayer in his personal life, and as a result, freely unites himself in thought and aspirations to the divine Benefactor upon whom he knows he depends for all that he is and all that he has. This becomes a constant, habitual intimacy with God, which urges him to turn his mind and heart to Him again and again throughout the day, if only for a second. For this type of person, prayer is as natural as breathing. To him it is a way of life, something which flows from the human nature God has given him—from his awareness of his own nothingness and the allness of his Creator.

You may ask the question—how is such prayerfulness cultivated? How does one freely get in this habit of union with God?

First of all, I must say that ordinarily it doesn't come simply by inspiration, but we have to work at it. We must be ever on the alert to realize that God is everything and the rest is nothing—without Him. This means, of course, that we must be willing to eject self from our life and let God occupy its place. It means that we must make every effort to look at life through the eyes of God Himself—seeing His estimate of things regarding time and space and all human activities of this world. It means looking up to God instead of looking down to earth, and having deeply implanted in our minds and hearts the goal and purpose God has in store for those who truly love Him. It means that in every temptation or sorrow, desolation or loneliness, we instinctively unite ourselves to God and ask His help. Saint Paul put it in capsule form, when he said, "So whether you eat or drink or whatever you do, do everything for the glory of God" (1 Cor 10:31).

Prayer means that we should have a sort of free, easy access to God, and not restrict ourselves with any set formula or type of prayer. What may be good for one with a certain temperament would not be good for someone else of a completely different type of disposition. And just as the body likes variety in the nourishment it imbibes, so the soul enjoys a different spiritual menu now and then. Some people always say the same prayers day after day, or after every Holy Communion, and don't feel quite right if they happen to omit some of these. Yet in doing this, they are restricting their own souls from further spiritual nourishment, which God is most eager to supply.

Wouldn't it be far better that while repeating these certain prayers, or even before commencing, I would take the one word "Jesus" and dwell upon His Holy Name for as long a time as I feel drawn to do so, even though this may be at the expense of my set prayers? Or must I keep my routine, no matter how boring it may be, and continue to say them?

To me the answer is clear. If I speak heart to heart with God, even for two minutes, my prayer is deeper and will have a greater effect on my spiritual life than all the routine vocal prayers in the prayer book. And it won't be long until I shall learn how, from that small beginning, God will draw me forward and teach me more and more. If I find that my mind wanders, or my heart is cold and unmoved, then I can always fall back on my set form of prayers to fill up what time remains.

Simplicity and childlikeness in our prayer is necessary if we are to discover the consoling value of this liberty of the children of God. Stereotyped forms of prayer, excellent and useful as they are, are best when they suggest this deeper praying from our own hearts and not when they chain us down to their wearying repetition. It would be far better to say, "Jesus, I love you," for an hour, if I could really mean it all the time, than to repeat the most perfect act of love spoken by one of the greatest saints in heaven. Perhaps my words would be fewer, weaker and more stammering, but Jesus would know that at least they are mine—and come right from my own heart.

Such a prayer as this sweeps away all interior unrest and is a safeguard against temptations. It opens the mind to higher things and leads to an inner knowledge of God. This habitual union with God cultivates our love of Him and causes it to grow stronger and more beautiful every day of our life. As a result, our life on earth is a happier one and far more successful, for it anticipates the life to come and becomes a foretaste of what God has in store for those that love Him.

Remember—the time may be delayed, the manner may be unexpected, but the answer is sure to come. Not a tear or secret sorrow, not a breath or holy desire poured out to God will ever be lost, but in God's own time and way will be wafted back again in clouds of mercy, and fall in showers of blessings on you, and on those for whom you pray.

God bless and keep you in His Sacred Heart now and forever.

45

Doesn't God Know
What We Need?

THE QUESTION IS OFTEN ASKED, "Why do we pray to God to grant us what we want or think we need? Doesn't He already know what we need and what is best for us already? Why keep storming Heaven for an answer to our difficulties, whether they are material or spiritual, since God already knows and has determined what will take place? How can we really change anything by our prayers? Hasn't God decided from all eternity what He is going to give us and what not? As the popular song has it, "Que sera, sera"—"What will be, will be!"

This does sound rather baffling to explain, but only when one doesn't understand how God looks at all finite earthly things in the light of eternity. It's true: God does know what is best for each one of us, even our most hidden needs, and once His divine plan is decreed from eternity, it is absolutely unchangeable. But does He still wish us to pray for what we need? Yes, He does. Why?

Since He created us after His image, endowing us with an intellect and free will, He expects us to act in an intelligent, free manner. He did not create us as robots or machines that always act in a certain way. He doesn't push a button and we react this way or that way, but He leaves us free to choose what we judge is best for us.

It is according to God's plan that He has also decreed that certain answers will be granted us only insofar as we ask for them. And even though the divine plan is absolutely unchangeable, God nevertheless has established it with the foreknowledge as to whether we would pray or not. In other words, with God there is no past nor future—all is one magnificent present. He has decreed to answer our prayers and give us what is best for us, because He at the same time knows that we will freely pray for our needs. If we didn't pray, then His will would be that these answers would not be granted, because we didn't cooperate with His grace and pray. It all depends on our free act what God determines to do.

No wonder then that our divine Savior taught most emphatically that we should storm Heaven with our prayers, asking, yes, but at the same time, leaving all things in His hands, because He knows what is best for us from an eternal viewpoint. He tells us, "Ask, and you shall receive; seek and you shall find; knock and it shall be opened unto you" (Mt 7:7–8). Christ continues to repeat to each of us as He spoke to His apostles, "If you ask the Father anything in My Name, He will give it to you" (Jn 16:23).

It surely follows, then, in God's eternal plan that humble, confident, persevering prayer is the necessary condition which He requires of all who expect to have their requests answered or their needs alleviated.

This becomes a little easier to understand if we look at the world of nature around about us. The bushes grow and bring forth fragrant, beautiful flowers, but only because someone has first planted the seeds in that particular garden. Now God knew and decreed from all eternity that these flowers would blossom and beautify the earth, but under the condition that the gardener would first plant the seeds. Otherwise there would be no growing bushes budding forth with luxuriant flowers.

So, if we expect our prayers to be answered, I would suggest that we pray as though all depends on God, and at the same time do all we can to help ourselves. It is not sufficient for us to pray and do nothing on our part to have our prayer answered. This would be presumption. We were always told in our studies to pray as though all depended on God, but to study as though all depended on ourselves. I can't help but think of the little California girl who was taking an examination in geography. Not being able to think of an answer to a particular question, she picked up the crucifix on her rosary and prayed, "Dear Jesus, please make Los Angeles the capital of California." With Sacramento the already established state capital of California, obviously God would not answer her prayer. She should have studied harder for her examination.

There is just one last point I would like to bring out while still on this subject of prayer—and that is to leave the answer in God's hands. We can't see very far and may be praying for something that if God granted it to us, our eternal salvation might be placed in danger, or some other catastrophe would occur. So, in this matter of petitioning I always say the best prayer is that of Christ in His agony in the garden, "Let this chalice pass from Me, but not My will, but Thine be done."

God bless and keep you in His Sacred Heart now and forever.

46

Confidence in Prayer

TO SOME PEOPLE, prayer may seem to be a waste of time, for it cannot change what's going to be. They say, "Wouldn't it be presumptuous on my part to think that my little prayer can change what will be?" It is true that my prayer cannot change what will be, but it will make come to pass what will be. For God in His divine Providence told us through the lips of His Eternal Son, Jesus Christ, "Amen, Amen, I say to you, whatever you ask the Father in My Name He will give you" (Jn 16:23);"Ask and you shall receive, seek and you shall find, knock and it shall be opened unto you" (Mt 7:7). In other words, it is in God's unchangeable mind that if we pray with confidence, He will bring about what is best in the light of eternity.

It is very encouraging and consoling to know that we have such a powerful force in prayer. Scientists seek to change the weather and control it. They endeavor to find means to reach the very planets in the heavens and control them, but in prayer, we have the means to control the destiny of our own soul. For by prayer, we control the very future in God's provisional plan. The divine Master Himself said, "Whatsoever you shall ask the Father in My Name He will give to you."

Now it is very important that we be confident in the use of this powerful means at our disposal. Without confidence, we don't really pray. For prayer is not mere words uttered; it is the expression of the heart that worships God. Without confidence, such prayer is enfeebled and dies, and there is not true worship. For the true meaning of worship is that the one puts a right value, a right judgement in his relationship to his Creator and acknowledges Him as such—as all truth, all goodness and all love. Certainly anyone aware of God as the very essence of all perfection has no reason whatsoever not to trust in Him. He is not an evil that we fear, One whom we are afraid to approach, and, as a result, run away from. He Himself is the good that we crave, the truth that we seek, and the love for which we yearn. And our prayer is not an effort to tell Him something that He doesn't already know. He has no need of our finite words to be informed of our needs. In prayer we simply manifest our dependence on Him, confident that He will give us all that is best for us and all that we need. He is ready to give, but we cannot receive unless we are in the attitude of prayer, and this means that we must have a prayerful mind and heart. That is why we say it is so important that we have confidence in prayer.

Without our realizing it, prayer actually shapes the future. Through prayer one controls the world. In a certain sense, through prayer one controls God, for when prayer is rightly made, whether it is in worship, thanksgiving, petition, or expiation, it must have the vital ingredient of confidence because each type of prayer expresses man's worship and recognition of God and His supremacy over him. Our divine Lord expressed this very thought on several occasions and in many parables when He said that we should be confident in prayer, knowing that our heavenly Father knows our every need.

One time He told of the man whose neighbor begged him, even after he had gone to bed, to come down, open up his bakery and give him a loaf of bread. The man insisted so persistently and confidently that finally out of sheer desperation, as it were, to get rid of him, the baker came down and gave him the loaf of bread. Christ concluded by saying, "Will not you fathers give bread when your children ask for it; for after all, you are good and love your children. How much more so will not your Heavenly Father give to each of His children what they ask for in confidence." And unlike the man in the parable, God is never unwilling to give. He is always wanting to share His goods with us. But in order to receive we must be in the attitude of prayer—we must know; we must ask; we must seek.

Are, there perhaps some prayers that one cannot have confidence in? Our Savior answers in the negative, for he said, "Whatsoever you shall ask the Father in My Name shall be given to you" (Mt 14:13). This is the only provision, that we ask with the power and authority of His divine Son, and in so doing we can rightfully say that there is no limit to what may be asked in prayer. But sometimes it seems that we don't get what we pray for. Should we then be discouraged? Surely here is the time when one has reason for not being confident in prayer. Take the example of the mother praying for the conversion of her son for years—all to no avail. Or the prayer of the man whose body is bloated with cancer. How can he pray with confidence, knowing that his prayer will be answered? In such cases as these confidence is absolutely necessary, for we have already said that true prayer is an expression of the worship of God—and that true worship is placing God's knowledge and God's will before our own. The truly confident man knows that his prayer is answered, even when he doesn't understand how.

For prayer is an act of worship and finds its perfection in an act of faith. So day after day, the good mother continues to pray for the conversion of her son, knowing that her prayer is a total trust in God, even when the fulfillment of that prayer seems impossible. And the suffering man afflicted with cancer does not find it strange that he continues to pray with confidence, for he knows his prayer is an expression of his trust in the eternal goodness of God's plan, and he doesn't want anything—much less a cure—if it doesn't fit in with what God wants. This is to pray with confidence.

God bless and keep you in His Sacred Heart now and forever.

47

The Laity and Prayer

THE LAST COMMAND that our divine Master gave to His Apostles before He ascended into Heaven from Mount Olivet was to go forth and teach all nations what He had taught them, and to baptize all in the Name of the Father and of the Son and of the Holy Spirit. He also told them that He would stay with them always even to the end of the world.

That command sent the Apostles Peter, James, Matthew, and the others, scurrying off to the far corners of the world—through Palestine, Syria, Asia Minor, through Macedonia, down to the tip of Greece, across the Adriatic to Rome itself, and further west into what are now known as Spain and France, even to Africa and far-off India. The Mediterranean Sea, once the stronghold of pagan Rome, within a few years became a Christian lake. Like a firebrand, Saint Paul, the great Apostle, set the world on fire with the love of the Savior. All felt the burning zeal of his words and the charity of his life, as he cried out, "The love of Christ urges me on." But, it was really the greatest teacher of all who was reliving His life in Paul as he spoke to Greek and Roman, Jew and gentile alike.

That same command of Jesus Christ has echoed down through the long corridor of centuries, calling upon other apostles to walk in the footsteps of Saints Peter and Paul and to go forth to teach all nations—down even to our own day. Each of us is called upon to be an apostle, to spread in this day of ours His kingdom here on earth.

"What," you say, "me an apostle? I can't be an apostle! I'm a lay person! I'm not a priest! I'm not going to the foreign missions. Why,

I've got my family to provide for. These children keep me plenty busy. I just haven't time for anything else. How can I be an apostle?"

This is just what I am trying to drive home to you! It's true you may not be able to go to the foreign missions and be another Saint Paul setting the world on fire with your preaching and teaching. You may never become a priest administering the sacraments or a sister or brother teaching His doctrine in the classroom. But each of us has the capacity and capability of becoming an apostle and doing great work for God in whatever state or walk of life we happen to be—an apostle of prayer. The laity are just as essential in this regard as we, the priests, brothers, and sisters. It doesn't make any difference whether we are married or single or consecrated to God; we can each of us make our way of life such that everything we do becomes a prayer to spread the mystical Body of Christ—His kingdom here on earth—to the farthest corners of the world.

It's not so much the what we do, but the why we're doing it that counts. And, the why is for the apostolic intentions of the Sacred Heart.

"That's all very wonderful," you say, "and sounds unbelievably beautiful. But, how can I—washing dishes, making beds, sweeping the walk, mopping the kitchen, driving a truck, pounding a typewriter, working behind a desk, lying sick on my back in bed—how can I have such a tremendous part in the important work that our divine Savior gave to the Apostles, to go forth and spread the good news of Christianity to help in the salvation of souls?"

Here's how! Each day, you offer up everything you do through the Morning Offering, praying for the same intentions burning in the Sacred Heart of Jesus. By means of this prayer you sanctify your complete day—and everything becomes an offering made to God, provided, of course, that you have his divine life in your soul through sanctifying grace. This not only brings you closer to God, but also helps countless others—the suffering missionary in China, the courageous apostle in Alaska braving freezing weather to bring knowledge of the Prince of Peace to the Eskimo, the sinner crushed beneath the wheels of an automobile to make one last prayer for mercy to God, your own children and those dear to you—to love God more. This is how we become twenty-four-hour-a-day apostles without going to the missions, without preaching sermons. The Morning Offering is like the golden touch of King Midas. Everything he touched turned to gold, so everything we touch—even in thought or desire, even eating, drinking, sleeping, or having fun—turns into spiritual gold, which the moth does not consume nor the rust corrode.

This is the way of life for the laity. This is the Apostleship of Prayer, the prayer of the Sacred Heart.

It doesn't make any difference whether one is wealthy or poor, sick or in health, beautiful or not, old or young, in the limelight or the background; by consecrating the day to the Sacred Heart, everything takes on eternal value.

This is a way of life for the laity! This is to be an apostle through prayer, the prayer of the Sacred Heart.

God bless and keep you in His Sacred Heart now and forever.

48

Communicating in Christ

WHILE ON THE SUBJECT of communicating in Christ, I think I should tell you about an episode in my own life which took place while I was engaged in giving a retreat in the Hawaiian Islands. I had never been there before, and now this gave me the opportunity of fulfilling a lifelong ambition—that of visiting the leper colony at Kalaupapa on the island of Molokai. Believe me, it was an unforgettable experience. To see these poor people being eaten away by this dreadful disease certainly gave me a deeper appreciation of the many gifts God had given to me, especially the health and integrity of my body.

I visited and communicated with several of these unfortunate people who were necessarily living in exile at the foot of the great, almost inaccessible cliffs, of Molokai. Here were men and women living out their days whose faces and bodies were not pretty to look upon exteriorly, but who were really radiating with the love of God in their souls. There was truly an inner type of communication among these men and women suffering the same sickness, enduring the same loneliness, bearing the same cross after Christ, in Christ, and for Christ. There was an understanding that went beneath the surface. It was not important what the outside appeared to be; all that really mattered was their union of thought and heart and inner feeling. Each one identified himself with the other, knowing that he, too, understood and had the exact same cross to carry. It was almost like the communication of the Son of God in becoming man. He became like him in all things: sufferings, joys, sorrows, trials, everything, and in so doing He could truly communicate with man, transforming him into Himself from within.

There was in particular a little old woman on her rocking chair who told me she had been there for thirty-nine years. She spoke in a sort of hollow way, because she had a tracheotomy in order to breathe. Her hands were really not hands at all—just two knobs on the ends of her forearms. Her face had been slowly eaten away and looked more like a living skull. She was also blind, her eyes turned back in their sockets. There was no nose at all; her teeth protruded through a mouth that had no lips.

Yes, it was quite a sight! But what made me realize the true beauty of this woman was the fact that her every living moment was a constant prayer in union with Jesus Christ suffering for her. About her neck hung a rosary which she said daily over and over again.

How did she do it? She couldn't hold the beads in her hands, because she didn't have any fingers! So she put the beads in her mouth and counted the Our Fathers and Hail Marys with her teeth. I'm sure you can well imagine the lump that came up into my own throat. I asked her what she prayed for, and her answer really thrilled me.

"My mission in life," she said, "is to pray for priests." Or course I immediately jumped at this beautiful expression of faith and said, "Please pray for me," and she answered that she would. I knew then that when she prayed for me she would also be praying for you because your intentions are also my intentions in the great Heart of Christ.

Then, to see the joy and interior happiness of the sisters who took care of these sick but wonderful people, dedicating their lives in acts of heroic virtue, gave me a new insight into the meaning of our divine Lord's words, "Whatsoever you do to the least of the brethren you do unto Me." Truly, these good women of the Gospel knew the real meaning of communicating in Christ—to give of self without counting the cost. They identified themselves so much with their patients that they really got inside their skins and thought and felt with them. They had learned that the secret of getting along with others is the ability of projecting oneself out of self and becoming one with the other. This is the divine touch that Christ Himself brought to man when He assumed human nature.

This is a basic principle in all relationships, especially regarding parents and children. Young people must learn that if they would find themselves, they must first look for others; if they want to be remembered, they must forget themselves; if they want to be heard, they must first listen; if they want to be understood, they must first attempt to understand. And, of course the same applies to parents. They must remember that being older and more experienced does not always mean they are infallibly correct in all circumstances, and that they too, even though they may be right, must be careful to make decisions justly but kindly.

Truly, only by this kind of communication in Christ can man in every state of life reap the full measure of earthly happiness—a foretaste of the eternal happiness God has in store for those that love Him.

God bless and keep you in His Sacred Heart now and forever.

49

Growing Older Graciously

IN ALL THE GOSPEL WRITINGS, there is none perhaps more familiar than the words which Jesus Christ spoke to those who would walk closely in His footsteps: "Learn of Me, for I am meek and humble of heart" (Mt 11:29) and "Unless you be converted and become as little children you shall not enter the kingdom of Heaven" (Mt 18:3). For those who find the years taking their toll, it is comforting to realize that they have many opportunities of putting into actual practice in their daily living these kindly words of the divine Master.

First of all, they should regard the length of their years as a treasured gift from the hand of God Himself, for the purpose of man's life here on earth—to be one with God in Heaven forever—does not change with the changing years! A long life simply means more ample time to establish in practice, as well as in theory, the teachings of Jesus Christ and the absolute necessity of saving one's immortal soul. As the advancing Christian plods through these declining years of his life, a particular interior attitude or habitual frame of mind ought to be deepening in his soul—that of detachment from all material, earthly things of time, and a more ardent longing for his Creator and the eternal kingdom which He has in store for those who love Him.

One of the most evident truths of all is the fact that every one of us is getting older minute by minute. We can live only one second at a time. No sooner do we say, "This is my second I am living," when that very second is gone—never to return! Whether we are bawling youngsters in a baby carriage or crippled oldsters in a wheelchair, we are all living the same moment at the same time. And, try as we may, none of us can ever live that same moment over again. In this sense, no one gets old. Everyone just gets older.

Isn't it logical then for all of us, particularly for the elderly, to take hold of those precious moments while they come and make the most of them, adapting ourselves to the changing circumstances that necessarily come upon us as the years pile up? Yes, truly, there is a way of growing older graciously and happily, but this does mean a great deal of childlike humility, patience, and courage.

There is a definite need for those growing older to be patient with themselves and with the young. When strength of body is gradually diminishing and the nervous system begins to show the wear and tear of the years, pain and disability begin to make themselves felt. All of this is part of God's plan to wean us away from the attractions of this world and draw us gently to Himself. When we find it difficult to do all we used to do, and to coordinate our muscles as in younger days, or to remember facts quickly and think clearly at times—all this daily dying to self can be sanctified, can be a purifying process for our soul when consecrated to the Sacred Heart as an offering in union with Christ dying on the cross. In fact, all the humiliations of old age cheerfully attuned to the loving will of God prepare us for the greatest moment of our life, when stripped completely of self we gasp our last breath and enter into the presence of our Creator.

It is comforting to realize, too, that if we have committed sins in the past, even serious ones, these very faults can be the source of our gaining merit: by our humble acknowledgement of these, recognizing ourselves as we truly are before God and by our being childlike in our sorrow for having offended our Best Friend, who loves us so much that He died with His Heart pierced for love of us. These particular sins may be bitter thorns in our crown of mental suffering, which press deeply into our minds and hearts as we look back upon a misspent youth, but actually, if we are humble enough to see ourselves as we are in God's eyes, be truly sorry for those sins, and have confidence in His infinite mercy and forgiveness, then these very sins can be our glory, happiness, and peace—oh, not the sins, but the repentance of them, the sorrow for having committed them.

It takes humility, too, for one of the many with long years of experience behind him to be patient with the imprudent, overzealous young, especially when they act as though they were the only ones ever to do or accomplish anything really worthwhile. At times like these, the wise oldsters have to bite their tongues and eat humble dirt in their effort to keep silent. But throughout it all, in the eyes of God they are gaining precious merits for a closer union with their Creator forever in Heaven.

In growing older graciously and humbly, such a person knows the truth about himself, about his position in the community of his fellow man, and about God. He knows that he is like a cell in the body. He depends on the whole body for his life. Without the community and its life-giving spirit, he becomes an outcast; he perishes. As a cell in the community, he has an important work to contribute to the health of the whole. He does this work well, no matter how humble it may seem to him or to others. In spite of his failings, his sins, he knows that God is his Father, that God loves him, that when he cries to the Lord, the Lord will hear his voice, that He will not despise his humble supplication. Realizing his nothingness with God, he casts all his care upon the Lord who sustains Him.

God bless and keep you in His Sacred Heart now and forever.

50

An Ever-Flowing Fountain

ONE OF THE MOST THRILLING EXPERIENCES of my life was the time I held the miraculously preserved right arm of the great missionary, Saint Francis Xavier, in my own arms. It happened some years ago, on the occasion when this precious relic was being carried to various places throughout the world for the public veneration of the faithful. One of the stops was the beautiful Blessed Sacrament Church in Hollywood, California. Thousands of people came from far and wide to see and reverence this four-hundred-year-old relic of a saintly man of God. (I'm sure you can imagine how breathtaking it was for me to be able to hold his arm in my own and ask his powerful intercession before the throne of God to help me in my priestly work here on earth, and to share with him the eternal joy of God's presence in Heaven.)

Then a blinding thought struck me like a bolt of lightning! What if we had only the right arm of Jesus Christ miraculously preserved in our midst? What vast crowds would turn out to see such a wonderful relic—the right arm of the Son of God Himself! It would probably be kept in the most sacred part of Saint Peter's in Rome. Pilgrimages would be organized and people would travel from all over the world to visit such a holy shrine. I'm sure it would be the lifelong ambition of every man, woman, and child to get even a momentary glimpse of this great gift of God to man.

Yet, pause for a moment! We not only have the right arm of our Savior, Jesus Christ—a part of His Body—but we have His complete Body, Blood, Soul, and Divinity! True—He is veiled under the external appearance of bread and wine, but that little white Host and that chalice of wine, after the words of consecration are pronounced during the Holy Sacrifice of the Mass, are no longer bread and wine, but the Body and Blood, the Humanity and Divinity of the Son of God! Mysterious, yes, but absolutely true on the Word of God Himself.

As we study the whole history of God's condescending love, never was it so transcendently clear than when Jesus Christ at the Last Supper gave to His Apostles and to the whole world His own Body and Blood to be their food and drink. It took God to be able to think of manifesting His love in such a way—to imprison Himself under ordinary bread and wine so that He could become a living, strengthening nourishment for man—a very part of Him. The eternal words of Jesus Christ leave no doubt of this, for He said, "He who eats My flesh and drinks My blood has life everlasting and I will raise him up on the last day. For My flesh is food indeed and My blood is drink indeed. He who eats My flesh and drinks My blood, abides in Me, and I in him" (Jn 54:56).

Here truly is the ever-flowing fountain for peoples of all nations and races to drink from and to be filled to overflowing with love and happiness. Here is a means of bringing peace and unity to everyone, for all are invited to this banquet table of the Lord to share the same spiritual food. The great Apostle, Saint Paul, expressed this very clearly when he said, "Because the bread (on which we feed) is one, we—many though we are—are one body."

The learned doctor of the early Church, Saint Cyril of Jerusalem, brought to light this same thought when he wrote, "The Eucharist is the 'act' of this all vivifying humanity; therefore, it is the sacrament of the Mystical Body, the Church. The Body of Christ produces in us what the Word effects in His Humanity; it transforms, vivifies, deifies us. Thus, through the Eucharist, Christ unites us in Himself with God and with one another." He goes on to say that the effects which the Humanity of Christ produced by a visible activity during its mortal existence, it now produces invisibly, but no less truly, in the Eucharist. "If mere contact with the sacred flesh of Jesus," he says,

> gives life to a dead body, should we not experience effects still more wonderful when we receive the sacred Eucharist? Surely it must completely transform those who receive into its own perfection;

that is, into immortality. Be not surprised at this; do not ask how it is possible. Think rather how water which, though cold by nature, seems to forget its nature when it is set upon the fire, and takes on the victorious energy of the fire. It is the same with us. Corruptible as we are in the flesh, we lost our own weakness by this "mingling" with the Eucharist, and we are transformed into what is proper to the Eucharist, that is, into life.

Truly, nothing, neither sickness nor distance nor all the subtle temptations and evil machinations of hell should ever close our ears to the quiet peaceful invitation from the tabernacle. "Come to Me, all you who labor and are burdened, and I will give you rest . . . This is the bread that comes down from Heaven . . . He who eats this bread shall live forever."

God bless and keep you in His Sacred Heart now and forever.

What if you could come even closer to Jesus?

Servant of God Cora Evans was a wife and mother, a convert from Mormonism, and a mystic who suffered the stigmata. Guided by a renowned Jesuit spiritual director, she wrote of her visionary experiences during ecstasy and vividly interpreted the word of God.

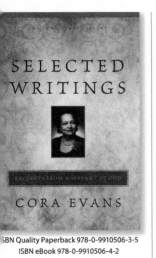

SELECTED WRITINGS

CORA EVANS

ISBN Quality Paperback 978-0-9910506-3-5
ISBN eBook 978-0-9910506-4-2

Now available in quality paperback book form: excerpts from her personal diary, meditation, and stories—plus homilies by Father Frank Parrish, S.J.

Cora was entrusted with the worldwide promulgation of the Mystical Humanity of Christ, a way of prayer encouraging the faithful to live with a heightened awareness of the living indwelling presence of Jesus in their daily lives (see 1 Cor 3:16). It is Eucharistic Spirituality directly linked to our role in fulfilling the mission of Christ (see Jn 17: 20-26).

The cause for Servant of God Cora Evans is underway.

Bookstore notice for wholesale pricing visit CoraEvans.com/bookstore

Selected Writings Imprimatur Most Reverend Richard Garcia, D.D. Bishop of Monterey, California, USA September 14, 2015

Prayer for the Intercession of Cora Evans Imprimatur Most Reverend George H. Niederauer Archbishop of San Francisco February 18, 2011

Request prayer cards for the Intercession of Servant of God Cora Evans Mike@CoraEvans.com or write to Mystical Humanity of Christ 735 28th Avenue San Mateo, California 94403

The Mystical Humanity of Christ *Publishing*

Purchase books at your Catholic bookstore or visit *SelectedWritings.CoraEvans.com*
Save 25% use promo code SAVE25